PATCHWORK OF DREAMS

UN MOSAICO DE SUEÑOS

梦幻组合

रंग बिरंगे सपने

א צוזאמענקומען פון חלומות

UN MOSAICO DI SOGNI

DIE BUNTE WELT DER TRÄUME

ΜΩΣΑΙΚΟ ΟΝΕΙΡΩΝ

AISLINGÍ PHIOSÁLA

Разноцветные мечты

فُسَيْفُسَاء من الأَحْلام

KOBIERZEC SNÓW

무지개의 꿈

UNE MOSAÏQUE DE RÊVES

MOZAÏEK VAN DROMEN

פסיפס חלומות

1

Write to us for our complete catalog. All books in print, from 1975 on.

The Spirit That Moves Us Press
P.O. Box 720820, Jackson Heights, Queens, N.Y. 11372-0820
(718) 426-8788

*"A well-deserved reputation for discovering new talent
as well as featuring better-known names... Highly recommended."*
—Library Journal

BOOKSTORES may order direct or from Ingram Book Co. (800) 937-8000;
Baker & Taylor Books (800) 775-1100; Bookpeople (800) 999-4650;
the distributors (800) 348-5200; Small Press Distribution (800) 869-7553

CLASSROOM or WORKSHOP orders: Teachers—request an examination copy,
which will become your free desk copy should you order ten or more copies.

INDIVIDUALS: If you don't see one of our books in your bookstore, ask that it
be special-ordered, or you can order direct from us. Along with your literary
bookstore, the following stores will special-order our books through the Barnes
& Noble Special Order Program: B. Dalton Bookseller; Doubleday Book Shops;
Scribner's Bookstores; Bookstop; Barnes & Noble Bookstores.

LIBRARIES may order direct or from Baker & Taylor, Blackwell North America,
or most other jobbers, as well as Small Press Distribution.

BOOKS IN THE CULTURAL DIVERSITY SERIES
No. 5—*Patchwork Of Dreams*
No. 4—*Speak To Me: Swedish-language Women Poets* (Swedish & English; poetry)
Jaroslav Seifert, Nobel Laureate (poetry; two in Czech & English):
No. 3—*Eight Days: An Elegy for Thomas Masaryk*
No. 2—*Mozart In Prague: Thirteen Rondels*
No. 1—*The Casting Of Bells* (English only; his first collection in the U.S.A.)

THE *EDITOR'S CHOICE* SERIES
Editor's Choice III: Fiction, Poetry & Art from the U.S. Small Press (1984-1990)
Editor's Choice II: Fiction, Poetry & Art from the U.S. Small Press (1978-1983)
Editor's Choice: Literature & Graphics from the U.S. Small Press, 1965-1977

First U.S. Publisher of a collection by Jaroslav Seifert, Nobel Laureate

The press is a member of the Small Press Center in Manhattan;
its editor is a member of P.E.N. (Poets, Essayists & Novelists).

This will be the last book that the editor will typeset on his obsolete, 8-kilobyte-
memory IBM Electronic Selectric Composer. From now on, with the tutelage of
Marcela Bruno, it'll be an Apple Macintosh.

PATCHWORK OF DREAMS

Voices from the Heart of the New America

Stories, Poems, Essays, Drama, Photographs & Interviews

Edited by
MORTY SKLAR & JOSEPH BARBATO
Assisted by Lisa Weinerman Horak

 The Spirit That Moves Us Press
Jackson Heights, Queens
New York City : 1996

Acknowledgements & Information

Mario M. Cuomo's piece is from his *Diaries Of Mario M. Cuomo*, Copyright ©1984 by him; reprinted by permission of Random House, Inc. Jaime Manrique's piece is from his *Latin Moon In Manhattan*, Copyright ©1992 by him; reprinted by permission from him and St. Martin's Press. Bharati Mukherjee's piece is from her *The Middleman And Other Stories*, Copyright © 1988 by her, and published by Grove Press; reprinted with the author's permission. Harvey Wang's photographs are from his *Harvey Wang's New York*, Copyright ©1990 by him, and were published by W.W. Norton; reprinted with the photographer's permission. Susan Orlean's piece, excerpted from her "All Mixed Up" in the June 22, 1992 issue of *The New Yorker*, is Copyright © 1992 by the author and reprinted with her permission and that of *The New Yorker*'s.

Number 5 of the Ethnic Diversity Series
This collection is Volume 12 of *The Spirit That Moves Us* (ISSN 0364-4014).
This First Edition was published in September 1996.

The Spirit That Moves Us is indexed in *The American Humanities Index*; *Index to American Periodical Verse*; *Short Story Index*; and *Poetry Index Annual*. Anthologies are indexed in *Granger's Index to Poetry* and *Modern Language Association International Bibliography*. Printed on acid-free paper with soy ink.

Grateful acknowledgement is made to the following for funds provided in support of the publication of this book:
    The National Endowment for the Arts, a federal agency
    The New York State Council on the Arts
    The Queens Council on the Arts
and to Norma Vogel, Peter and Dorothy Rinaldo, Richard Kovac, Ad Hoc Translations (for typesetting the foreign languages on the half-title page), and the Kamber Group (for Karen Thompson's visual for the "Following The Thread" section).

Library of Congress Cataloging-in-Publication Data:

Patchwork of dreams : voices from the heart of the new America /
    edited by Morty Sklar & Joseph Barbato ; assisted by Lisa Weinerman Horak.
        p.   cm. — (Ethnic diversity series ; no. 5)
    Includes bibliographical references.
    Summary: A multicultural collection of stories, poems, essays, drama, and photographs by past and current residents of Queens, New York.
    ISBN 0-930370-43-0 (pbk. : alk. paper) : $12.50. — ISBN 0-930370-44-9 (pbk. : signed A-Z : alk. paper) : $25
    1. American literature—New York (N.Y.) 2. Ethnic groups—New York (N.Y.)—Literary collections. 3. Queens (New York, N.Y.)—Literary collections. 4. American literature—Minority authors. 5. American literature—20th century. [1. American literature—New York (N.Y.)—Collections. 2. Queens (New York, N.Y.)—Literary collections. 3. Ethnic groups—Literary collections.] I. Sklar, Morty, 1935- . II. Barbato, Joseph, 1944- . III. Series.
PS549.N5P37 1996
810.8'09747243—dc20   92-42702
                                                                          CIP
                                                                          AC

PREFACE

by Morty Sklar & Joseph Barbato

MORTY SKLAR

When I moved back to Jackson Heights, Queens, New York City in 1989 after having lived in Iowa City, Iowa (population 50,000) for eighteen years, I understood what my mother, born in 1900, had been telling me: "I feel like I'm living in a foreign country."

I noticed that many businesses had a poster in their windows, whose words,

JACKSON HEIGHTS
THE REAL MELTING POT
OF AMERICA

were framed by the flags of sixty-four nations. That poster made me feel proud of my neighborhood, and the poet and publisher in me envisioned a collection of poems from as many of those countries as possible.

I stopped by Joe Barbato's small, packed office on the other side of Roosevelt Avenue and the number 7 Flushing-to-Times-Square "Immigrant Express" elevated train tracks that are the border between Jackson Heights and Elmhurst, where I had grown up and Joe had lived for the past twenty years. I said, "Joe, how does this sound?: a book titled *The Real Melting Pot Of America: Poems from Jackson Heights*." Joe explained how this was no longer a melting pot the way it was when our families had come from "the other side." He also said, as a writer of prose in the midst of writing a book about Elmhurst, "Why not *Jackson Heights/Elmhurst/Sunnyside/Woodside*?"

Eventually, we decided on all of Queens, and had gone from *Melting Pot* to *Great Mosaic* to prose-writer Joe's poetic *Patchwork Of Dreams*.

We saturated the Queens and New York City media with our news-release that stated we wished to see stories, essays and photographs from as many ethnic backgrounds and races as we could get, from residents and former residents of Queens. It was the compulsive part of me that also placed a classified ad in the national *Poets & Writers Magazine*, but the results of that (almost half our submissions came from outside of Queens and New York) caused me to see my compulsive nature in a more positive light.

Julia Alvarez, who's been living in Vermont, said in a note that she didn't have any prose for our purposes, but she enclosed a wonderful poem. We then changed our subtitle to include *Poems*.

More poetry arrived, without our having announced that we were now considering poetry for the collection. My favorite note accompanying poems was from Joan Dobbie, now living in Oregon: "As a very small child I lived in Jamaica.... I'm just realizing that you didn't actually ask for poems, nor am I absolutely sure that Jamaica is in Queens. Near Queens maybe?" Her poem leads-off this book.

Susan Montez, who was living in Virginia but is back in Astoria, Queens, said in her note that accompanied her work, "Your call for manuscripts in *Poets & Writers Magazine* did not include poetry; nevertheless, I am sending you some poems." We liked her ten-pager enough to publish it here.

Then we received a play, "Homeboys," which we liked, and then Joe did some interviews and our subtitle was getting too long, so we changed it to its present form.

Another "happy accident": We'd been anticipating the publication of an article/interview that *New York Newsday* did on this project while we were still looking for manuscripts. The piece did not appear in the issue where we expected it, *but* what did appear there was a big spread on Harvey Wang, illustrated with his swell photographs of people at their old (some obsolete) professions, and when we contacted him to ask permission to publish some of them, he said yes.

One of the things we realized when we started to receive manuscripts for *Patchwork Of Dreams* was, some of them had little to do with present-day America/Queens. But then we thought, even the pieces whose settings are twenty, thirty, forty and fifty years in the past, are about the *New America*—of their time: Mario Cuomo's father digging ditches, then his parents opening a grocery store with their savings. Julia Alvarez's family, the first Hispanic one to settle in their neighborhood. A. J. Cipolla's characters coming to terms with blacks and whites attending the same school. Joan Dobbie, a child who didn't know the language of her new country. Rodlyn Douglas, a black immigrant experiencing racism—from other blacks. Thomas Kennedy, whose characters are Irish but whose American experience is universal. Rudy Kikel, whose foreignness was his sexual orientation. Silvio Martínez Palau, whose characters range from those who would never try to fit in, to those who abandon their identities to try to do so. Virginia Montero Seplowin, whose barbershop setting, date situation, and mother's vision for her future cross all boundaries of ethnicity. Barbara Unger, whose Jewish and gentile characters live-out a war between Americans even as America is at war in Europe and Asia. Harvey Wang, whose images portray individuals at now rare or obsolete or eternal occupations (blacksmithing, pinsetting, flavored-ices-making).

In the new America of 1907, my father at ten years of age got off the boat from Russia. In 1910, his father died and my father went to work to help support his mother and younger sister and brothers. In 1928 he and a partner had a suite of rooms in a hotel, where they saw their customers in the woolen industry. They were each making a whopping $300 a week. In 1929 the woolen industry was one of the first to crash, and my father bought a barrel of peanuts and a box of cellophane bags, stapled them to cardboard holders, and peddled them. Then he went to work in a hardware store where the owner asked him if he knew how to install a lock. He never had, but said yes, and was sent to an apartment to do so. When his boss came to check on the installation, he said to my father, "Good job, Jack, but when you put in a lock, it's easier to put the strike in first."

Someone else was impressed by my father—by how clean

and manicured his nails were (a hangover from his better days) while he was setting up a display in the hardware store window. That was my mother, who he'd not yet met. A few years later, three years before I was born, my father was using my mother's parents' basement to stock some hardware "joblots" that he'd bought at an auction and was selling to retail stores. As far back as I can remember, my father was leaving for work at his one-man business at 7, 7:30 a.m. and returning home about twelve hours later. Saturdays he might start out at 8, 8:30 and return at 6:30, 7. Sundays he sometimes went to his store for a few hours. In the evenings and on Sunday you wouldn't catch him in front of the tv without a stack of paperwork on his lap.

In 1966, my Marcela left her Andean city of Arequipa, Peru, and came to her new America. In that year, two months earlier, I had left an old America behind, and came into my new, drug-free America.

In the new America of 1996, my Korean neighbors, John and Lana, open their small grocery store at 9 a.m., a couple of hours after John picks up their fresh produce in his van at the Manhattan markets, and they close at 9:30 p.m.—an improvement over the first five years I'd known them, when they opened at 8 a.m. and closed at 10:30 or 11 p.m.—unless they were busy selling goods, at which time they might stay open until 11:45. And of course, when the big new market-and-delicatessen first opened a block from their store, John and Lana began opening at 7:30 a.m., before the new market, and closing at 10:30 p.m., a couple of hours after the new market closed.

Most of the little guys who stay in business are the ones who work two weeks in one—*and* have some good luck. *That* new America hasn't changed in my lifetime.

JOSEPH BARBATO

This book is a literary evocation of a place and a time. The place is Queens, a borough of New York City. The time is now. The subject, seen through the prisms of many writers, is America and immigrant dreams.

Why Queens? Because it is the most ethnically diverse area in the United States, and because its immigrants from Asia and Latin America are producing fiction, poetry, and other writing of interest to readers everywhere. Cities across the country— Los Angeles, Miami, Chicago—are changing rapidly amid the present third world immigration. None has the extraordinary mix of people now found in the two-million-population outer-borough called Queens.

There, beginning in the shadow of the 59th Street bridge linking Queens to Manhattan, people from 120 nations who live in Astoria, Sunnyside, Woodside, Jackson Heights, Elmhurst, Flushing, and other Queens neighborhoods are writing the latest chapter in the American story. Roger Sanjek, a social scientist at Queens College of the City University of New York, has given this new chapter a name: The Great Transition.

"The United States is beginning a Great Transition; by the end of the 21st century it will be a 'majority minority' nation," observes Sanjek. "The Census Bureau projects that in the year 2100 the U.S. will be 10% Asian, 17% black, 28% Hispanic, and 46% white. Queens *now* offers us a glimpse of this future."

Fortunately, Queens has gifted writers who are giving voice to life in the heart of the new America. They are working in a fine tradition. Many outstanding writers have grown up or lived in the borough: novelists from Jack Kerouac to Paul Bowles, Toni Morrison, Mary Gordon, and E.L. Doctorow; journalists Jimmy Breslin and Art Buchwald; essayists Lewis Thomas and Stephen Jay Gould. Yet few authors have drawn on the borough for material, with the exception of Breslin, whose semi-fictional lowlifes put Queens Boulevard on the literary map; and Gordon, whose novels capture Queens' Irish. Perhaps Queens, for some, was simply a quiet place to write, or a place to leave behind.

9

This is not so for the writers in *Patchwork Of Dreams*. They have found inspiration for their poetry and fiction *in* the borough; in the transition taking place in their neighborhoods. Their "foreigners" and "minorities" are not abstractions drawn from debates on multiculturalism. They are individuals like you and me, fumbling, reaching, struggling to survive and get ahead.

I have met many Colombians and Dominicans in Queens, but have seldom known them as rendered in Jaime Manrique's "Colombian Queens" and in Julia Alvarez's "Jamaica, Queens, 1963." I have often walked along 74th Street in Jackson Heights, but only now truly see the richness of the Asian Indian community described in Clark Blaise's "Beyond the Bridge and Tunnel."

Perhaps this first-of-its-kind anthology will make you see the familiar in a new light, too. If so, it will be because these poems and stories move us. They show life lived. They say something about which we care.

I hope the pieces in our Patchwork grab you. I think some will toss you across the room.

For my mother
and
In memory of my father, Joseph M. Barbato
1912-1992

and with special thanks: to Dusty,
whose love and encouragement sustain me,
in this and in all adventures, including the Queens years;
to Lisa, whose energy and enthusiasm helped shape
these pages; and to Morty, for asking me, and for all the fun.

In memory of my mother, Selma Sklar
1900-1995

and in memory of Leonard Randolph,
daddy of the small-press N.E.A. programs, and good guy

A Marcela, mi media naranja

and to Harris Drake, who first turned me on to poetry,
and who helped me to know where I came from.

Contributors in Alphabetical Order

Salimah Ali
Julia Alvarez
Joseph Barbato
Mohamad Bazzi
Clark Blaise
Javier Castano
Hsiang-Shui Chen
A. J. Cipolla
Norman Clarke
Mario M. Cuomo
Dept. of City Planning
Joan Dobbie
Rodlyn H. Douglas
Didi DubelyeW
Ed DuRante
Rhina Espaillat
Audrey Gottlieb
Darryl Holmes
Lisa Weinerman Horak
Thomas E. Kennedy
Rudy Kikel
Yala Korwin
Corky Lee
David Low
Jaime Manrique
Maureen McCafferty
Susan Montez
Bharati Mukherjee
Mark Nickerson
Susan Orlean
Silvio Martinez Palau
Roger Sanjek
Daniel Schweikert
Virginia Montero Seplowin
Morty Sklar
Barbara Unger
Harvey Wang

TABLE OF CONTENTS

13

FOLLOWING THE THREAD
Edited by Lisa Weinerman Horak

Norman Clarke
Daniel T. Schweikert
Virginia Montero Seplowin
Mohamad Bazzi
Mario M. Cuomo
Silvio Martínez Palau
Joseph Barbato/interviews with neighbors

Susan Orlean
Department of City Planning
Roger Sanjek
Hsíang-Shui Chen
Rodlyn H. Douglas

Harvey Wang, photographer

Joan Dobbie
JUST OFF THE QUEEN ELIZABETH
New York City 1948

I was thin as a waif,
just two and a half,
our tiny brown
courtyard with its tiny
brown sandbox
were huge.
              Somebody's
mother's head
protruded from a high
distant window
surrounded by brick.
              I heard
the word, "watermelon," saw
its lush pink,
tasted the meat.
              Later
my sister
brought home
(rich black on white paper)
"the alphabet." We fought,
it tore.
              Once I was
standing alone outside
the vast gaping mouth
of our door.
              In the courtyard
were children. I called out
the only two words
I could think of in English,
"GO AWAY!"
              I meant
for the children to come,
I was longing
              to touch them.

Corky Lee, photographer

20

Bharati Mukherjee
DANNY'S GIRLS

I was thirteen when Danny Sahib moved into our building in
Flushing. That was his street name, but my Aunt Lini still
called him Dinesh, the name he'd landed with. He was about
twenty, a Dogra boy from Simla with slicked-back hair and
coppery skin. If he'd worked on his body language, he could
have passed for Mexican, which might have been useful. Hispanics are taken more seriously, in certain lines of business,
than Indians. But I don't want to give the wrong impression
about Danny. He wasn't an enforcer, he was a charmer. No
one was afraid of him; he was a merchant of opportunity. I
got to know him because he was always into ghetto scams that
needed junior high boys like me to pull them off.

He didn't have parents, at least none that he talked about,
and he boasted he'd been on his own since he was six. I admired that, I wished I could escape my family, such as it was.
My parents had been bounced from Uganda by Idi Amin, and
then barred from England by some parliamentary trickery.
Mother's sister—Aunt Lini—sponsored us in the States. I don't
remember Africa at all, but my father could never forget that
we'd once had servants and two Mercedes-Benzes. He sat
around Lini's house moaning about the good old days and
grumbling about how hard life in America was until finally
the women organized a coup and chucked him out. My mother sold papers in the subway kiosks, twelve hours a day, seven
days a week. Last I heard, my father was living with a Trinidad
woman in Philadelphia, but we haven't seen him or talked
about him for years. So in Danny's mind I was an orphan,
like him.

He wasn't into the big-money stuff like drugs. He was a
hustler, nothing more. He used to boast that he knew some
guys, Nepalese and Pakistanis, who could supply him with anything—but we figured that was just talk. He started out with
bets and scalping tickets for Lata Mangeshkar or Mithun Cha-
kravorty concerts at Madison Square Garden. Later he fixed

beauty contests and then discovered the marriage racket.

Danny took out ads in papers in India promising "guaranteed Permanent Resident status in the U.S." to grooms willing to proxy-marry American girls of Indian origin. He arranged quite a few. The brides and grooms didn't have to live with each other, or even meet or see each other. Sometimes the "brides' were smooth-skinned boys from the neighborhood. He used to audition his brides in our apartment and coach them—especially the boys—on keeping their faces low, their saris high, and their arms as glazed and smooth as caramel. The immigration inspectors never suspected a thing. I never understood why young men would pay a lot of money—I think the going rate was fifty thousand rupees—to come here. Maybe if I remembered the old country I might feel different. I've never even visited India.

Flushing was full of greedy women. I never met one who would turn down gold or a fling with the money market. The streets were lousy with gold merchants, more gold emporia than pizza parlors. Melt down the hoarded gold of Jackson Heights and you could plate the Queensboro Bridge. My first job for Danny Sahib was to approach the daughters in my building for bride volunteers and a fifty buck fee, and then with my sweet, innocent face, sign a hundred dollar contract with their mothers.

Then Danny Sahib saw he was thinking small. The real money wasn't in rupees and bringing poor saps over. It was in selling docile Indian girls to hard-up Americans for real bucks. An Old World wife who knew her place and would breed like crazy was worth at least twenty thousand dollars. To sweeten the deal and get some good-looking girls for his catalogues, Danny promised to send part of the fee back to India. No one in India could even imagine *getting* money for the curse of having a daughter. So he expanded his marriage business to include mail-order brides, and he offered my smart Aunt Lini a partnership. My job was to put up posters in the laundromats and pass out flyers on the subways.

Aunt Lini was a shrewd businesswoman, a widow who'd built my uncle's small-time investor service for cautious Gujarati gentlemen into a full-scale loan-sharking operation that financed half the Indian-owned taxi medallions in Queens. Her rates were simple: double the prime, no questions asked. Triple the prime if she smelled a risk, which she usually did. She ran it out of her kitchen with a phone next to the stove. She could turn a thousand dollars while frying up a *bhaji*.

Aunt Lini's role was to warehouse the merchandise, as she called the girls, that couldn't be delivered to its American destination (most of those American fiances had faces a fly wouldn't buzz). Aunt Lini had spare rooms she could turn into an informal S.R.O. hotel. She called the rooms her "pet shop" and she thought of the girls as puppies in the window. In addition to the flat rate that Danny paid her, she billed the women separately for bringing gentlemen guests, or shoppers, into the room. This encouraged a prompt turnover. The girls found it profitable to make an expeditious decision.

The summer I was fifteen, Aunt Lini had a paying guest, a Nepalese, a real looker. Her skin was white as whole milk, not the color of tree bark I was accustomed to. Her lips were a peachy orange and she had high Nepalese cheekbones. She called herself "Rosie" in the mail-order catalogue and listed her age as sixteen. Danny wanted all his girls to be sixteen and most of them had names like Rosie and Dolly. I suppose when things didn't work out between her and her contract "fiance" she saw no reason to go back to her real name. Or especially, back to some tubercular hut in Katmandu. Her parents certainly wouldn't take her back. They figured she was married and doing time in Toledo with a dude named Duane.

Rosie liked to have me around. In the middle of a sizzling afternoon she would send me to Mr. Chin's store for a pack of Kents, or to Ranjit's liquor store for gin. She was a good tipper, or maybe she couldn't admit to me that she couldn't add. The money came from Danny, part of her "dowry" that

he didn't send back to Nepal. I knew she couldn't read or write,
not even in her own language. That didn't bother me—guaranteed illiteracy is a big selling point in the mail-order bride racket—and there was nothing abject about her. I'd have to say
she was a proud woman. The other girls Danny brought over
were already broken in spirit; they'd marry just about any freak
Danny brought around. Not Rosie—she'd throw some of them
out, and threaten others with a cobra she said she kept in her
suitcase if they even thought of touching her. After most of
my errands, she'd ask me to sit on the bed and light me a cigarette and pour me a weak drink. I'd fan her for a while with
the newspaper.

"What are you going to be when you finish school?" she'd
ask me and blow rings, like kisses, that wobbled to my face
and broke gently across it. I didn't know anyone who blew
smoke rings. I thought they had gone out with black-and-white
films. I became a staunch admirer of Nepal.

What I wanted to be in those days was someone important,
which meant a freedom like Danny's but without the scams.
Respectable freedom in the bigger world of America, that's
what I wanted. Growing up in Queens gives a boy ambitions.
But I didn't disclose them. I said to Rosie what my Ma always
said when other Indians dropped by. I said I would be going
to Columbia University to the Engineering School. It was a
story Ma believed because she'd told it so often, though I knew
better. Only the Indian doctors' kids from New Jersey and
Long Island went to Columbia. Out in Flushing we got a different message. Indian boys were placed on earth to become
accountants and engineers. Even old *Idi Amin* was placed on
earth to force Indians to come to America to become accountants and engineers. I went through high school scared, wondering what there was in my future if I hated numbers. I wondered if Pace and Adelphi had engineering. I didn't want to
turn out like my Aunt Lini, a ghetto moneylender, and I didn't
want to suffer like my mother, and I hated my father with a
passion. No wonder Danny's world seemed so exciting. My

mother was knocking herself out at a kiosk in Port Authority, earning the minimum wage from a guy who convinced her he was doing her a big favor, all for my mythical Columbia tuition. Lini told me that in America grades didn't count; it was all in the test scores. She bought me the SAT workbooks and told me to memorize the answers.

"Smashing," Rosie would say, and other times, "Jolly good," showing that even in the Himalayan foothills, the sun hadn't yet set on the British Empire.

Some afternoons Rosie would be doubled over in bed with leg pains. I know now she'd had rickets as a kid and spent her childhood swaying under hundred pound sacks of rice piled on her head. By thirty she'd be hobbling around like an old football player with blown knees. But at sixteen or whatever, she still had great, hard, though slightly bent legs, and she'd hike her velour dressing gown so I could tightly crisscross her legs and part of her thighs with pink satin hair ribbons. It was a home remedy, she said, it stopped circulation. I couldn't picture her in that home, Nepal. She was like a queen ("The Queen of Queens," I used to joke) to me that year. Even India, where both my parents were born, was a mystery.

Curing Rosie's leg pains led to some strong emotions, and soon I wanted to beat on the gentlemen callers who came, carrying cheap boxes of candy and looking her over like a slave girl on the auction block. She'd tell me about it, nonchalantly, making it funny. She'd catalogue each of their faults, imitate their voices. They'd try to get a peek under the covers or even under the clothing, and Danny would be there to cool things down. I wasn't allowed to help, but by then I would have killed for her.

I was no stranger to the miseries of unrequited love. Rosie was the unavailable love in the room upstairs who talked to me unblushingly of sex and made the whole transaction seem base and grubby and funny. In my Saturday morning Gujarati class, on the other hand, there was a girl from Syosset who called herself "Pammy Patel," a genuine Hindu-American Princess of the sort I had never seen before, whose skin and voice and eyes were as soft as clouds. She wore expensive dresses and you could tell she'd spent hours making herself up just for the Gujarati classes in the Hindu Temple. Her father was a major surgeon, and he and Pammy's brothers would stand outside the class to protect her from any contact with boys like me. They would watch us filing out of the classroom, looking us up and down and smirking the way Danny's catalogue brides were looked at by their American buyers.

I found the whole situation achingly romantic. In the Hindi films I'd see every Sunday, the hero was always a common man with a noble heart, in love with an unattainable beauty. Then she'd be kidnapped and he'd have to save her. Caste and class would be overcome and marriage would follow. To that background, I added a certain American equality. I grew up hating rich people, especially rich Indian immigrants who didn't have the problems of Uganda and a useless father, but otherwise were no better than I. I never gave them the deference that Aunt Lini and my mother did.

With all that behind me, I had assumed that real love *had* to be cheerless. I had assumed I wouldn't find a girl worth marrying, not that girls like Pammy could make me happy. Rosie was the kind of girl who could make me happy, but even I knew she was not the kind of girl I could marry. It was confusing. Thoughts of Rosie made me want to slash the throats of rivals. Thoughts of Pammy made me want to wipe out her whole family.

One very hot afternoon Rosie, as usual, leaned her elbows on the windowsill and shouted to me to fetch a six-pack of tonic and lemon. I'd been sitting on the stoop, getting new tips from Danny on scalping for an upcoming dance recital—a big one, Lincoln Center—but I leaped to attention and shook the change in my pockets to make sure I had enough for Mr. Chin. Rosie kept records of her debts, and she'd pay them off, she said, just as soon as Danny arranged a green card to make her legit. She intended to make it here without getting married.

She exaggerated Danny's power. To her, he was some kind of local bigwig who could pull off anything. None of Danny's girls had tried breaking a contract before, and I wondered if she'd actually taken it up with him.

Danny pushed me back so hard I scraped my knee on the stoop. "You put up the posters," he said. After taping them up, I was to circulate on the subway and press the pictures on every lonely guy I saw. "I'll take care of Rosie. You report back tomorrow."

"After I get her tonic and a lemon," I said.

It was the only time I ever saw the grown-up orphan in Danny, the survivor. If he'd had a knife or a gun on him, he might have used it. "I give the orders," he said, "you follow." Until that moment, I'd always had the implicit sense that Danny and I were partners in some exciting enterprise, that together we were putting something over on India, on Flushing, and even on America.

Then he smiled, but it wasn't Danny's radiant, conspiratorial, arm-on-the-shoulder smile that used to warm my day. "You're making her fat," he said. "You're making her drunk. You probably want to diddle her yourself, don't you? Fifteen years old and never been out of your Auntie's house and you want a real woman like Rosie. But she thinks you're her errand boy and you just love being her smiley little *chokra-boy*, don't you?" Then the smile froze on his lips, and if he'd ever looked Mexican, this was the time. Then he said something in Hindi that I barely understood, and he laughed as he watched me repeat it, slowly. Something about eunuchs not knowing their place. "Don't ever go up there again, *hijra-boy*."

I was starting to take care of Danny's errands quickly and sloppily as always, and then, at the top of the subway stairs, I stopped. I'd never really thought what a strange, pimpish thing I was doing, putting up pictures of Danny's girls, or standing at the top of the subway stairs and passing them out to any lonely-looking American I saw—what kind of joke was this? How dare he do this, I thought, how dare he make me a part of this? I couldn't move. I had two hundred sheets of yellow paper in my hands, descriptions of Rosie and half a dozen others like her, and instead of passing them out, I threw them over my head and let them settle on the street and sidewalk and filter down the paper-strewn, garbage-littered steps of the subway. How dare he call me *hijra*, eunuch?

I got back to Aunt Lini's within the hour. She was in her kitchen charring an eggplant. "I'm making a special *bharta* for you," she said, clapping a hand over the receiver. She was putting the screws on some poor Sikh, judging from the stream of coarse Punjabi I heard as I tore through the kitchen. She shouted after me, "Your Ma'll be working late tonight." More guilt, more Columbia, more engineering.

I didn't thank Aunt Lini for being so thoughtful, and I didn't complain about Ma not being home for me. I was in a towering rage with Rosie and with everyone who ever slobbered over her picture.

"Take your shoes off in the hall," Lini shouted. "You know the rules."

I was in the mood to break rules. For the first time I could remember, I wasn't afraid of Danny Sahib. I wanted to liberate Rosie, and myself. From the hall stand I grabbed the biggest, sturdiest, wood-handled umbrella—gentlemen callers were always leaving behind souvenirs—and in my greasy high-tops I clumped up the stairs two at a time and kicked open the door to Rosie's room.

Rosie lay in bed, smoking. She'd propped a new fan on her pillow near her face. She sipped her gin and lime. *So*, I thought in my fit of mad jealousy, he's bought her a fan. And now suddenly she likes limes. Damn him, *damn* him. She won't want me and my newspapers, she won't want my lemons. I wouldn't have cared if Danny and half the bachelors in Queens were huddled around that bed. I was so pumped up with the enormity of love that I beat the mattress in the absence of rivals. Whack! Whack! Whack! went the stolen umbrella, and Rosie bent her legs delicately to get them out of the way. The fan teetered off the pillow and lay there beside her on the wilted, flopping bed, blowing hot air at the ceiling. She held her drink up tight against her nose and lips and stared at me around the glass.

"So, you want me, do you?" she said.

Slowly, she moved the flimsy little fan, then let it drop. I knelt on the floor with my head on the pillow that had pressed into her body, smelling flowers I would never see in Flushing and feeling the tug on my shoulder that meant I should come up to bed and for the first time I felt my life was going to be A-Okay.

Harvey Wang, photographer

Harvey Wang, photographer

Thomas E. Kennedy
BLISS STREET

I was born on Bliss Street in Sunnyside, just down from White Castle Hamburgers—ironic names for a place that crouched in the hulking shadow and din of the el tracks. The IRT Flushing line rattled past overhead every ten minutes or so, when it was on schedule, usually just as Perry Mason was about to make a crucial revelation to Della Street.

We lived in the finished basement of a two-family house owned by two astygmatic brothers named David and Wilfred Darling. My little brother Dennis used to joke about their names and their affliction in a quavering falsetto: "oh, David, darling! oh, Wilfred, darling!" He also used to do a routine of the astygmatic David directing the astygmatic Wilfred as he steered his big beige 1954 Plymouth, which we called The Brown Cow, into the driveway.

The Darling brothers finished the basement themselves and rented it out illegally. We had two bedrooms and a living/dining room beneath a seven-foot ceiling. The pipes, of which there were many, were boxed and the walls panelled in grain-masked plywood, and just outside the water closet was a metal shower stall whose walls rumbled like radio thunder if you bumped them. The windows, at the top of the walls, looked out on the tires of the Darlings' Plymouth parked in the alley.

My brother and I were only allowed to invite kids home in good weather when we could play in the yard and my mother could give us a snack at the old redwood lawn table. The Darlings did not care for us playing in the yard. They worried we disturbed the second-floor tenants, who liked to keep the glass doors of their balcony open. "Afraid the kids'll drown out the el," my father said. My mother thought they were afraid people would notice a third family was living there.

"It's against the fire laws," she said.

My father, in his arm chair reading the sports pages of the *Daily News*, grunted.

"They don't want us to be seen at all," my mother said.

"They'd like the boys to stay hidden away down here all day in this, this . . ."

My father looked at her. His face was mild, but she stopped speaking. She smirked, rolled her eyes.

Dennis and I were lying on our stomachs on the floor, playing cars. The purple carpet had a series of borders which served as highways, and our little metal roadsters cut right angles around the corners of the rug. The floor beneath us vibrated as the Flushing line rumbled past out above Roosevelt Avenue —named not for Franklin, but for Teddy. Dennis had a toy motorcycle cop tied to the bumper of his car and was dragging him along the purple carpet road, uttering a low murmur of agony. The MC cop, which he called Flynn, was made of flesh-colored flexible plastic that smelled like a cheap shower curtain. Flynn was the hero of all Dennis's games. Dennis put him through great adversity—he would be bound, hung, scalded with matches, buried to his neck in the dirt of the yard and painted with honey to attract the little red ants or the big black ones, but always, when the odds were worst, Flynn would break free, overpower his enemies, survive, prevail, triumph.

Even though Dennis was two years younger than I, his games always seemed more original and interesting than mine. When he wasn't around, sometimes I would co-opt his plots, but I was too proud to do it in front of him. After all, I was the big brother. He should imitate me.

My mother was twenty-nine years old, a very pretty, dark-haired woman, and I feared she regretted having married my father, a short balding red-head who was five years older than her and drove a laundry truck for a living. My father was a joker, always had a quick, dry retort, but my mother didn't smile much anymore, and she never let him forget why. She didn't have to say much, just a phrase once in a while, muttered with her back to him, while she did the dishes. "A basement. Live in a basement. What my mother must think."

He would look up from his paper or the tv, say, "Got some-thin' in your eye, Beth?" He could usually make her laugh with a crack like that. But she didn't smile now. She didn't even answer. "What'd you say anyhow?" he asked, although we all knew very well what it was, and she wouldn't repeat it.

I didn't mind so much living there. The only thing I really wished was that there could have been windows in the little bedroom where Dennis and I slept, but if they only looked out on somebody's dirty firestones, what would be the difference?

Dennis and I knew every inch of our home and we had no real complaints. We knew the places where the plywood had separated from the white-limed walls and you could put secret messages written in candle wax on typing paper that you made look old by scorching the edges with a matchflame. We knew about the empty alcove behind the curtain and the secret closet there that led into the furnace room, and we knew about the crawlspace under the front porch, a wonderful, terrifying place closed off with a woodskid on hinges, bolted shut.

Dennis and I also knew a secret; the bolts were not anchored fast, but could be jerked out and the wood skid opened onto a dark, earth-floored cavity. We peered into the darkness to try to imagine what was there: buried treasure, jewels, arrowheads, old pirate pistols, a corpse. We shone the long aluminum five-battery flashlight in, but you couldn't see much, just the rumpled dirt floor and dungeon-grey walls.

What I especially liked about the crawlspace was that it scared Dennis more than it did me. One day as we were peering in, I told him I saw something move in there, something big. "I'm going in for a look," I said. He started to cry, begged me not to, and his terror was so exquisite I just had to have more. I hoisted myself up onto the sill, and in one push was in. I heard him crying out, running, and then suddenly I was inside in the cool dark quiet, the soft damp earth beneath me, my nose full of the musty, grave-like smell.

Stupidly, I didn't think about who Dennis would run to for help, but just about the time he was coming back with my mother, I felt something crawling inside my pants leg.

I screamed. Dennis screamed.

"Be still!" my mother screamed. "Stop that screaming! Oh, God! What's happening in there!"

She reached in and grabbed hold of my foot, dragged me out through the dirt, got me down on the floor, and started shaking me by the shoulders, hollering into my face, "I thought I told you *never* to ..."

"There's something crawling inside my pants!" I yelled to make her stop. Dennis ran into the shower stall and pulled the curtain after him, while my mother, alternately screaming, slapping, laughing, hugging me, unbuckled my belt and pulled off my pants.

Her search of my clothes produced two large black beetles which she sealed, alive, into a mailing envelope to show my father when he got home from work. Further, I was ordered to dress again in my dirt-smudged clothes and sit in a chair in the hall; I was not permitted to wash myself until my father had a chance to see with his own eyes.

"I wouldn't have got so dirty if you hadn't pulled me out through the dirt like that!" I hollered.

But she didn't even seem to hear me. She paced and muttered to herself, went around wiping out clean ashtrays, scrubbing the sink, the shower stall (Dennis was now out in the yard reading a Beetle Bailey comic and munching cornflakes from the box).

"This is it," she said. "This Is It. A basement. A *cellar*. Insects. *Insects!*"

I knew what she meant by the word insects. She meant the unspeakable thing which happened only to filthy undesirable humans.

"They're *not* cockroaches!" I said. "They were just ordinary everyday beetles, water bugs."

"You *shut* your mouth!" she hissed, and her eyes fixed me in a way that made me frightened.

It was only about an hour before my father got home. When

he climbed down out of his laundry van, my mother was waiting for him up the stairs by the side door that led into our apartment.

My father was still wearing his grey laundry driver's uniform and had the grey cap tipped back on his bald red pate.
"Hah!" he said when he saw my mother standing there at the
door. "What do you know? The royal welcome, hey? Where's
the red carpet?"

"This is no joke, *buster*," she snapped. Buster was a serious
word with my mother. "Go down and take a look at your *oldest* son."

I could see my father's face before he saw me as he came
down the narrow stairway, saw the look on his face saw that
he expected to find me minus an eye or with a hand torn open
from a cherry bomb, or wrapped in a body cast or something.
When he got down to the little place at the foot of the stairs
that my mother, with dripping sarcasm, called *the foyer*, he
stopped and saw me there, all smeared with dirt, and I saw the
startled relief in his eyes. "Jingo netties," he said, "You look
like the wreck of the hesperas."

I started to laugh, but my mother was already on him. "Do
you know where he got that way? Do you know what was *on*
him?" She had the sealed envelope in her hand and was tear-
ing back the flap. My father looked from her to me to the furnace room door.

"Beetles," he said, peering into the envelope at the half-
dead waterbugs.

"*Insects!*" she said. "Cockroaches!" And, "You *filthy* Irish
failure! This is what you provide for us!"

Then there was silence. I waited for some evil word from
him, some word I had never heard him speak before, but which
would be the likely response: *Bitch. Slut.* Or worse. But he
said nothing to her. To me, he said, "Go wash your face, son."
Then he turned and went back up the stairs. I heard the door
of his laundry truck smack shut and the engine start, and then
I was alone with my mother.

Dennis lingered at the foot of the stairs. He made a face at me. "Puke for brains," he whispered, "It was *your* fault."

"Wouldn't have happened if you didn't call *Mom*," I said. "*Baby* ass."

When my father wasn't back by eight, my mother served dinner without him. We ate our fishcakes in silence, and afterwards watched *Palladin* and *Gunsmoke*, and my mother let us stay up all the way to the late news, when my father was still not back.

I woke sometime during the night to the rattle of a key in the door upstairs, listened intensely for whiskey sounds, but there were none. I reached beneath the bed for my Baby Ben alarm clock. The luminous dial said it was two-fifteen. The basement was quiet but for the sounds of his footsteps, slow, but not heavy like they would be if he had gone over to Ryan's as he did once in a while to drink shots of rye and talk and sing old songs with the men and women there.

When I woke in the morning, he was gone again, his truck was gone. My mother said, "Your father came home very late and had to leave early today."

"When's he coming back?" I asked.

"He has some things to do," she said. I recognized the evasion, asked no more. I hated to go to school that day, hated leaving Dennis alone with my mother, the two of them with their dark hair and fine features and little feet, hated going off on my own, a round-faced little redhead whose father was god knew where. They were two of a kind, and I was my father's boy, as everybody said, except my father was gone somewhere. I recall it was a spring day, the first day that year I noticed buds on the hedges and trees. It was only my ninth spring so I did not yet recognize this as the triumph of life over death, was not yet able to recognize that we had just been through the dead of winter, the long bleak stretch between Christmas and Easter, did not realize that the good weather was coming again or identify my parents' behavior as the strain of being cooped up all those weeks with kids who could not invite friends home and could not go out to play in the yard, being locked in a basement which made my mother think constant-ly of shame and failure, comparing our situation with her par-ents', her sister's and brother's.

At nine, you do not yet know that things change, that things can *be* changed. All I knew was that there were buds on the hedges, the sky was blue, the air mild on my face, my mother and father were fighting and it was my fault.

When I got home from school at three, my father's truck was parked outside the house. Its panel doors were wide open, and a striped mattress stuck out of it. On the sidewalk were a pile of planks that I suddenly recognized as the frame of my own bed.

Dennis was sitting at the redwood table in the yard, playing with his collection of ice cream sticks. He opened his mouth to speak, but I pressed the heels of my hands over my ears. I could not bear to hear it from him. I had to have it straight from Mom and Dad. That way, maybe I could make them change their minds. I ran down the cellar stairs to find my father standing in front of our dining table, which lay on its back, like a beetle, legs up in the air. He was screwing the legs off, one by one.

"Where's Mom?" I asked.

"She'll be right back."

"What are you doing?"

"I'll tell you all at the same time when she gets back."

I joined Dennis at the redwood table. One of the Darlings watched us through the kitchen window, his eyes crossed and his little moustache knotted above sour puckered lips.

"Screw him," I muttered.

"Oh yeah?" said Dennis. "You want to get us in even *more* trouble?"

"Wasn't my fault in the first place!"

"Was, too!"

My father appeared at the top of the basement stairs with the big round table top in his outstretched arms, hugged close to his body. That table had been my mother's mother's, one of the three pieces of furniture she was really proud of. The way he was carrying it you could see some kind of label pasted underneath, where the wood was not finished. It made you feel good the way the paper looked, yellow, kind of antique. It made you think of the past, of grandmothers and grandfathers, visits and all.

Gingerly, my father rested the table on the tops of his shoes, not to scratch it, just as my mother came into the yard carrying two brown paper A&P bags.

"What's going on here?" she demanded.

My father said, "We're moving. Bought us a house. Up on 34th Avenue. There's a tree outside."

My mother smiled the way she did only when she was very perplexed. "A *house*?" she said. "Who would sell *you* a house?"

From the sidelines, Dennis and I watched. "She shouldn't of said it like that," I whispered.

"Don't be so touchy," Dennis said. "She didn't mean it like that."

My father said, "I got a mortgage."

My mother's smile grew increasingly lopsided. "A mortgage? On what you make?"

"Hey," he said, "This guy at the bank, this Mr. Fowler, he looks at my baby blues, and he says, 'Oh, well, Mr. Duggan, so you got your down payment, do you? Well, that's fine, then.'"

My mother stared off at the Darlings' apple tree, the one that got twisted by Hurricane Alice the summer before, and without even looking at my father, she said, "Where'd you get the down payment, big shot?"

"She shouldn't have said it like that," I said.

"She didn't mean it that way," Dennis said, but he was as scared as me, I could tell, especially because she asked it without looking at him.

My father shifted the table on his shoes. He was looking

down at the pavement, and he was smiling the way he did when you knew there was no discussing something. Anybody from the outside who saw him would think he was smiling merrily, but both Dennis and I could see the smile and knew it meant something drastic. Maybe my mother did, too. Maybe that's why she wasn't looking at him. Her smile disappeared. She was no longer perplexed. Now her mouth was small, her pretty dark eyes even bigger than usual, and she stood with her legs apart but the toes of her scuffed loafers pointed in toward each other. "How will you ever pay it?" she whispered. "How will we eat?"

He took out his handkerchief and wiped his forehead. He was looking down the alley now, toward the laundry truck, and I could see he was getting ready to lift the table top again, that he was through talking. He dipped his knees and lifted the heavy round oak piece. When he had it up in his arms again, and his knees locked, he said, "I'll be working nights for a while. I got some extra hours over at Elmhurst General."

We slept in our own house that night, a red brick row house up on 84th Street between 34th Avenue and Northern Boulevard. There were trees spaced along the street, and you couldn't hear, smell, or feel the el train running along the tracks sixteen blocks southwest. Our neighbors on the one side were a lawyer named MacPhillips—the family name was written in metal script, built right into their front screen door—and on the other side a single man, a chiropodist named Dr. Digit.

It was a tall, narrow house, and Dennis and I each got our own bedroom, on the third floor, with windows that looked out to our own yard, which had trees and bushes and a rusted swing set. But Dennis came in and slept in my bed that night anyway, so we could discuss the meaning of these events. I didn't see that there was anything wrong. Mom was sore, but she had her own ideas about things, and I couldn't see that there was anything but good going on there. But Dennis thought Dad borrowed the money from this guy we knew about named Tony Beggs who lived in Corona and who would break somebody's legs for you if you paid him fifty dollars. This scared me pretty good. Tony Beggs was also a collector, and I had seen a film called *The Kiss of Death* about people like that which showed what Richard Widmark did to people who failed to keep up with the interest payments on the loans made to innocent family fathers in tight situations.

"You know what they do?" Dennis said. "They push old ladies in wheelchairs down the stairs. They set fire to your house and they beat up your father in an alley."

I said, "They file the silver fillings out of your teeth, too," trying to make a joke out of it, but I was pretty scared there in the dark in our new house, and the presence of my little brother's body in the bed with me didn't help much. I ran through it over and over in my head as I lay there, studying the new ceiling above my face. First I ran through the idea that it was not at all what we feared, that nothing bad was going to happen, that Dad had just taken a loan and had to work a couple extra hours a week over at Elmhurst General. But after I ran through that in my head, all the other possibilities still waited, things that had to do with shadows and alleys and Tony Beggs who had a nose that looked like it had been creased by wearing a tight heavy rubber band around it. I saw him pushing my father, hitting him, and I couldn't stand it, I couldn't picture it, tried to go back to the other idea where nothing was wrong, but it wasn't easy to keep that alive.

The truth of the situation was different, maybe worse in a way. My father had taken a loan from a bonafide finance company that had a little office on 37th Avenue run by a guy with a pencil moustache who drove around in one of those insect-looking German cars. The interest on the loan sounded like it was very low, but the thing is, it was paid out by the month, so really you were paying more than twenty percent a year.

This meant my father drove the laundry truck every day from eight-thirty to four-thirty, came home to eat and take a nap and was at the hospital from six in the evening till one in the morning. By not taking any meal break, he did it in a seven-hour shift, and he got paid ten percent extra for working nights.

"It's a deal," I heard him tell my mother. "All they want's that and my left nougat, and we're home free." My mother was not amused.

Apparently he ate on the move, while he worked, carried apples and bananas and left over boiled potatoes in the tool pockets of his workpants. He had a voracious appetite, but we didn't get much meat to eat anymore. We ate a lot of spaghetti and potatoes for dinner, and I can still remember the expression on my father's face when he looked at what was on the table, and the way he looked afterwards when it was all eaten up and he refilled his glass of water and took another slice of Wonder bread and looked from bowl to empty bowl. As hungry as he always was, he lost weight, and I could tell my mother was worried. She used to make baloney sandwiches for him to take to the hospital. Sometimes, when he was really tired, he got forgetful, and I would have to go over to the hospital to bring the food to him because he left the brown bag on the hall table.

Usually he was having a smoke outside the glass doors on Elmhurst Avenue when I got there, and I would hand over the bag, hang around with him there for a few minutes and shot the bull while he ate. He always offered me a piece of the baloney sandwich. I felt a little bit like I was visiting him in jail or something. After a few minutes, he'd flip away the butt of his cigarette and go his way inside the building, and I'd go my way down Elmhurst Avenue to Roosevelt, up 84th to our brick row house, where my mother sat alone in front of the tv, knitting or darning while Dennis did his homework at the dining table.

She looked so lonely there, kind of dazed, and the house was so quiet all the time now, without my father's jokes. Sometimes I even missed the sound of their arguments. She was much easier with Dennis and me during those first months, but it wasn't much of a relief because we knew it was not because she loved us more, but just because she was too confused or hurt to get mad.

One time when I brought the food bag over to my father, he wasn't outside waiting for me, so I went in to look for him. I saw him in the hall between the elevator banks shoving a bucket. It was on wheels and had a wringer in it. He pulled the mop up through the wringer so grey water squeezed out of it, then slapped the wet mophead onto the tile floor and started mopping. I stepped behind a pillar, my heart beating, to watch him there, a short, red-headed balding man in a white uniform shoving a mop through an empty hallway. Somehow, I hadn't known that was his job there. I remembered once or twice he took me on his rounds in the laundry truck when I was eight years old. It was fun. I felt proud to sit up in the front of the truck with him, help him lift out the folded clean laundry wrapped in neat brown-paper packages, enjoyed how he joked with all the people where he made pick-ups and deliveries. But in the hospital, I didn't see him with anybody. He was alone with his bucket and mop in an empty corridor slopping up dirt.

I hurried away after giving him his food and never went inside the hospital again. I feel ashamed to admit it, but it bothered me, too, that others might see him there like that. My friends, the neighbors. What would Judge MacPhillips think if he saw his next-door neighbor pushing a mop along a hospital corridor, mopping up other people's shoe filth?

My mother didn't much like it either, but for other reasons. She never saw him anymore, only on weekends, and half the time, he slept most of Saturday away. When he wasn't sleeping, he worked on the house. It was in bad shape, which is why he got it so cheap. The windows needed putty and sanding and paint. It needed paint everywhere. The wiring was bad, and the plumbing was set to go, piece by piece. The roof needed patching, and the yard was a mess.

It got to where Dennis and I didn't want to be home on the

weekends anymore. It was the same thing every week. My father on a ladder, scraping, sanding, painting, hammering, trying to get us to run after tools for him or down to the hardware store, or hold something or clean up after him, and all the while my mother would be in and out of the doorway to holler at him to let it be, forget it, sit down and relax and stop wasting his time on this broken down wreck that nobody but he would be so stupid to buy.

Usually he wouldn't answer. Sometimes he'd say, "You wanted a house. You got a house."

"I never said I wanted a house. You could of just rented a decent apartment."

"Rent. Sure. Throw your damn money out the window."

Then there were long periods where no one spoke at all in the house, only me and Dennis. I don't honestly know which was worse, the silence or the yelling.

That was how our life got to be then. I only remember it in little takes. My mother at the kitchen table peeling something, her eyes staring off, out the window at the yard. My father in his armchair in the half-furnished living room, elbows on his knees, staring at the floor, or snoring in front of the tv. He was skinny now, so his grey laundry uniform hung on him, and one time, on a Saturday evening, he went out for a walk without his shoes on. He walked in his sock feet down the middle of the road along our street. I went down to tell my mother about it, but she was sitting alone in the living room with just a single lamp lit, rubbing cold cream into her hands, and I didn't know what to say to her.

So I went back upstairs and sat by the front window and watched the street. About an hour later, I saw my father coming back. One of the men he used to go to Ryan's with, a blond round-faced man with a deep voice, was walking with him, leading him by the arm, walked him up to the door and rang the bell, then went away again.

The holidays were not much relief either, Christmas, Easter, summer vacations. There was never enough of anything except silence, which there was too much of. I actually got to dislike Christmas for a while, would get a sick feeling in my stomach hearing Gene Autrey sing "Rudolph the Red-nosed Reindeer" on the radio in the quiet house while my mother put together the old Christmas tree that she kept in a cardboard box in the attic.

Then one Christmas eve, my father put a little box under the tree with a tag that said "To Mom" on it, and when she opened it up, there was just a piece of paper inside, folded in four, with printing and some kind of rubber stamps on it.

"What's this?" she said. Her eyes had dark circles under them, and there was grey now in her dark hair.

"It's the loan I took for the down payment."

"So? That's a present?"

"It's paid up. I don't have to work nights anymore. Not unless you want me to take another year so we can buy some more furniture."

And that was the end of it. Dennis was twelve. I was fourteen. We had a father again. Mom had Dad again. And we owned a house.

It had seemed like forever, but really it was only five years, it only took five years to pay off that loan, and it changed everything for us. That was the first time I ever really saw that you could do things, change things.

All this happened thirty-five years ago. We never talked much about it when it was finally over. Then last year, Dennis and I came together again in Jackson Heights to close up the house, after we buried Mom. Dad had died of a heart attack two years before, and then Mom got sick pretty soon afterwards, and we came together with our own wives and kids to bury her in the plot at St. John's.

The house was valued at just about fifteen times what my father had paid for it, a small fortune. It would mean all the difference for my children and their education, for my life, and surely for Dennis's, too.

As we left the brick row house for the last time, I looked

back at it and said, "Boy, Dad really fixed things up for us."

"Dad? He would never have done a thing without Mom egging him on. We'd still be in that damn basement on Bliss Street."

For a moment, an old, bitter anger began to rise in me. I looked into my brother's dark, fine-featured face, coarsened some by the years, but still the same face I had bickered and laughed with through all the years we were kids. I was about to say something to him, something mean, but then I ran my hand through my thin red hair, thought, The heck with it.

That's just my brother for you. We never could agree about anything.

Julia Alvarez
JAMAICA, QUEENS, 1963

Everyone seemed more American
than we, newly arrived,
foreign dirt still on our soles.
Watched at first, by year's end
we were melted into the block,
owned our own mock Tudor house.
Then the house across the street
sold to a black family.
Cop cars patrolled our block
from the Castellucci's at one end
to the Balakian's on the other.
We heard rumors of bomb threats,
a burning cross on their lawn.
(It turned out to be a sparkler
left over from fourth of July.
Still, the neighborhood buzzed.)
The barber's family, Haralambides,
our left side neighbors, didn't want trouble.
They'd come a long way to be free!
Mr. Scott, the retired plumber,
and his plump midwestern wife,
considered moving back home
where white and black got along
by staying where they belonged.
They had cultivated our street
like the garden she'd given up
on account of her ailing back,
ailing legs, poor eyes, arthritic hands.
She went through her litany daily,
politely my mother listened,
Ay, Mrs. Scott, que pena!
her Dominican good manners
still running on automatic.
Until the day at the grocery

some old lady called her, *Spic!*
Mami spit back, *Old Bag!*
The Jewish counselor next door
had her practice in her house;
clients hurried up her walk
ashamed to be seen needing.
(I watched from my upstairs window,
gloomy with adolescence,
and guessed how they too must have
polite mothers, old world fathers,
foreign dirt pearling their souls.)
Mrs. Bernstein said it was time
the neighborhood opened up.
(She remembered the snubbing they got,
the first Jews on the block,
a few years back from Mrs. Scott.)
But real estate worried her,
our houses' plummeting value.
She shook her head as she might
at a client's grim disclosures.
Too bad the world works this way.
The Irish girl playing piano
down the street abruptly stopped
in the middle of a note.
I completed the tune in my head
as I watched the front door open
of the house across the street:
a dark man in a business suit
and a girl about my age
walked quickly into a car
that whisked her away to school.
(We Catholics had the day off—
an immaculate conception.)
Driving by, the girl looked up.
My hand lifted but froze.
On her dark face beyond glass

I had seen a look I remembered
from the days before we melted
in the United States of America:
It was hardness mixed with hurt.
It was knowing we never could be
the right kind of Americans.
A police car followed their car.
Down the street, curtains fell back;
blinds, slanted open, closed.
Haralambides left for work,
slamming his front door—
another fight with his pale wife.
Mrs. Scott swept her walk
as if it had just been dirtied.
Then the Irish piano commenced
downward scales as if tracking
the plummeting real estate.
One by one I imagined the houses
sinking into their lawns,
the grass grown wild and tall,
endless fields no one yet owned
swept by winds blowing across
the uncharted Atlantic
no foreigner had yet crossed
dreaming of a free country
others would have to pay for
once it was put on the market.

Javier Castano, photographer

50

Jaime Manrique
COLOMBIAN QUEENS

I had known Carmen Elvira and Olga since our immigration to Jackson Heights; but Irma, the other member of the Colombian Parnassus, was a more recent acquaintance. They published *Colombian Queens*, a monthly magazine that my mother always saved for me. It was distributed free, financed through ads taken out by Colombian restaurants, travel agencies, and grocery stores in the Jackson Heights area. Carmen Elvira wrote the gossip column; Olga was in charge of the horoscope and the Colombian recipes, and Irma, who worked as a teller in a Wall Street bank, wrote the business column. The rest of the articles were reprints, exclusively about Colombia. The middle section of the magazine—which was the bulk of it—was packed with photographs of Colombian show biz personalities in the New York area (the women usually in bathing suits), and pictures of people recently deceased and girls in their *quinces*, etc.

On more than one occasion, Carmen Elvira had invited me to submit a section of my Columbus poem for consideration, but I had repeatedly turned down her request. Without consulting me, five poems of my book *Lirio del Alba* had been reprinted with many typographical mistakes. For a long time after that, I forbade Mother to mention Carmen Elvira's name in my presence.

I was about to ring the bell of Olga's home when the door opened and the hostess greeted me with kisses on both cheeks. The pleasant smell of burnt eucalyptus hit my nostrils. Walking down the wide-planked hall carpeted with cowhides, I experienced deja vu: I felt as if I were in a house in Bogota. Every detail was Colombian—the furniture, the pictures on the walls, even the plastic flowers.

I greeted Carmen Elvira and Irma, who were sitting on a couch drinking *tinto*, the espresso-like demitasse that Colombians swill nonstop. The air-conditioning was on and the curtains drawn, so that the room was in semidarkness, giving the scene a vaguely conspiratorial atmosphere. The three women,

who ranged in age from their late forties to midfifties, differ-
ed sharply in appearance: Carmen Elvira, who was from the
Cauca Valley, was tall and her complexion and features Med-
iterranean in color and shape; Irma, who was from Pasto, was
on the short side, stocky, and her features were Incan. She
wore her hair in a crew cut and was dressed in bermudas and
sandals.

Olga, who was from Bogota, was extremely petite and a natural blond. She was dressed in a sleeveless white cotton dress
and wore high heels. It was spooky how, because of their close
association, they seemed, at least in spirit, three weird sisters.

I was offered, and accepted, a *tinto*. Without asking for my
preference, the hostess put two heaping spoonfuls of sugar in
the inch-and-a-half cup. I decided to be gracious and drink it
this way for fear of being labeled a gringo. The three women
looked at me with curious but benign expressions.

"May I smoke a cigarette?" I asked in Spanish.

"*Si, si, por supuesto*," Olga said in her tinny voice, pushing
an ashtray on the coffee table in my direction. It was made of
red clay and had the Colombian flag painted on it.

"We don't smoke anymore," Carmen Elvira said. "The
group's New Year's resolution was to give up smoking."

"Thank God and the Holy Virgin," Irma said, and crossed
herself.

Feeling like a criminal, I puffed on my Newport.

"How's Lucy?" Olga asked.

"She's fine thank you," I said. Then, remembering I was
among Colombians, I asked, "And how's your husband?"

For the next five minutes we inquired about each other's
parents, husbands, brothers and sisters, children, and even pets.
By then I had finished my cigarette and the sickeningly sweet
tinto. It occurred to me that good manners required that I ack-
nowledge the dubious honor of being elected a member of The
Colombian Parnassus.

"Don't mention it," beamed Carmen Elvira as the unack-
nowledged spokesperson of the group. "We have to move with

the times, and welcome the new generation."

"Personally, I'm not very fond of modern poetry. I prefer the old poets like Carranza. Ah, those sonnets. Do you love Carranza?" Irma asked me.

"Yes, I do." Like all Colombian children I had learned Carranza's poems in school, and did, indeed, favor his exuberant romanticism.

"The Sonnet to Teresa," Olga sighed, full of nostalgia for the poetry of the past.

Olga and Carmen Elvira looked at Irma beseechingly. Her expression becoming devout, Irma began reciting the sonnet:

> *Teresa, en cuya frente el cielo empieza,*
> *como el aroma en la sien de la flor.*
> *Teresa, la del suave desamor*
> *y el arroyuelo azul en la cabeza.*

Her eyes closed, her hands resting on her considerable breasts, Irma finished reciting the famous sonnet, which I will not endeavor to translate for you because its beautiful rhymes and music demand a greater translator than I could ever hope to be. When she finished, the women sighed and burst into applause. I joined them.

"That's poetry," Olga pronounced.

Carmen Elvira pontificated, "That's what I call great poetry."

"That's what I call love," elaborated Olga. "It's not enough to be a great poet. Oh, no. That's too easy. To write poetry like that, one must love very deeply and be a great lover. Like . . . like . . . Petrarch. I hope some day you'll write a sonnet like that to your girlfriend, Sammy."

Unsure of how to respond, I said, "I hope so too."

"By the way," Irma interjected, "do you have a girlfriend?"

I assumed a blank expression and said nothing. It was one thing to join the Parnassus, but to have my life scrutinized by these ladies was out of the question.

"Yes, he does," Carmen Elvira said, to my astonishment. "Lucy told me all about it, Sammy."

"All about what?" I said.

Carmen Elvira flashed a maternal, approving smile. "About you and Claudia."

"Claudia!" I exclaimed, for the second time that day.

"Claudia Urrutia?" asked Irma in disbelief, giving me a long, searching look. "She's so . . ."

"So wealthy," said Carmen Elvira to settle the issue.

"Hey, look," I said, to no one in particular. "I—"

"I hope you don't mind my mentioning it," Carmen Elvira interrupted me, "but Lucy told me you're practically engaged, that you're proposing tonight at the Saigon Rose."

"Congratulations, honey!" exclaimed Olga, leaping from the couch. "This calls for a celebration. I have an *aguardiente* bottle I've been saving for a special occasion. Excuse me, I'll be right back."

"I'll help you with the glasses," Carmen Elvira offered, getting up too.

"We might as well have our lunch after the toast," Irma threw in. "I'll serve the *pasteles*. You do like *pasteles*, don't you?" And, without waiting for confirmation, she followed the rest of the Parnassus into the kitchen.

I could have killed my mother. I reached for the telephone, but in the middle of dialing her number, I changed my mind. "Maybe I'm dreaming," I blurted out. I shook my head in an effort to wake myself up. But dreams are odorless and I could smell the *pasteles*. The situation reminded me of something; I couldn't, though, tell quite what. *Rosemary's Baby*, *Macbeth*, and *The Trial* all came to mind. I wondered if Claudia had been let into this plot, or whether we were both just random bystanders snarled in the machinations of a bunch of crazed Queens matrons.

Toasting my induction to the Parnassus, we drank the *aguardiente* Colombian style—a small glass filled to the top, followed by a quarter of a lime soaked in salt, which I chewed until my teeth felt as if they would fall out. Tears choked my vision. Carmen Elvira proposed another toast to my imminent engagement. I figured it would be better to play along than to go into long explanations about my and Claudia's sexuality. We drank to love and happiness. I had never seen Colombian women drink *aguardiente*: it is essentially a man's drink, but then, I reasoned, I was among intellectuals, not conventional housewives.

My body temperature had shot up at least ten degrees. The ladies produced their fans and proceeded to cool themselves, their mouths open and blowing air as if to take off the sting of the *aguardiente* on their gums.

"How about another *aguardientico*, Sammy?" Olga said.

"No, no, thanks. Maybe later." I felt the insides of my stomach cooking.

Irma started giggling. Carmen Elvira and Olga joined in, and together they became hysterical.

"What?" I asked, feeling uncomfortable. "What is it?" They were certainly not being very polite.

"You should see the color of your face," Irma cackled. "It looks red like ... guava paste."

"Like a brick out of the oven," Carmen Elvira chuckled, pouring herself another *aguardiente*.

I realized I had to put an end to the alcohol consumption before they became uncontrollable.

"I'm hungry," I said, pointing at the tray of aluminum foil-wrapped *pasteles* on the coffee table.

Irma unwrapped a *pastel* and served it to me on a plate, with a napkin and fork. It looked delicious; a steam cloud heavy with the aroma of vegetables and meats and corn traveled up my nostrils.

"Dig in, honey," Carmen Elvira said. "Don't wait for us; we made them just for you."

"I love corn *pasteles*," I said, putting a piece of moist chicken in my mouth. "Ummm, it's wonderful." Closing my eyes, I chewed slowly. When I opened my eyes, the three women were leaning over the table, serving themselves.

"Ah," Olga exclaimed, setting her plate on the table and pressing her lips on the napkin. "I forgot the drinks. Now, Sammy, since you're the guest of honor, what would you like to drink with your lunch?"

"I don't know," I said, wondering what kind of exotic Colombian fruit juice or brew she had to offer. "What do you have?"

Opening her eyes wide and looking at the ceiling, she counted with her fingers. "Let's see: Diet Coke . . . ginger ale, Tab, Perrier, grapefruit juice, and beer."

I asked for a Classic Coke.

Carmen Elvira ordered a Heineken.

"For me too," said Irma. "Nothing goes better with a *pastel* than a Heineken."

While the hostess went to get the refreshments, I made small talk, asking, "Who made the *pasteles*?"

"I did," Irma said proudly.

"I never thought it would be possible to make a *pastel* taste like they do in Colombia. But they taste just as if you had cooked them in banana leaves," Carmen Elvira said.

"This is the best *pastel* I've had in a long time," I complimented the cook.

"Thank you, *su merced*. Have another."

"I will, when I finish this one. It's so big."

"Yes, Irma makes the most generous portions," Carmen Elvira said. "I follow your recipe, my dear, but they just don't taste the same."

"There must be something you're leaving out."

"Obviously. But I wonder what it is. I cook the pork with the chicken in the scallions and tomato sauce."

"Do you use fresh or dry coriander? That makes a big difference."

"Fresh. And I sprinkle the coriander on the meat just before I wrap the *pastel* in the aluminum foil."

"Maybe you don't use enough *guascas*."

"That's it. The *guascas*! Why didn't I think of it before? But it's impossible to get *guascas* in Jackson Heights."

"I bring it from Colombia. But you know they don't allow fruits or vegetables or spices into the country. I have to hide it in my panties. Once, I had to eat an *anon* at JFK because they were going to confiscate it. So, I said, 'Please, let me eat it.' And I did."

"I remember you told me. It was an *anon* from your mother's yard. I wish I had the guts to do something like that. Nerves of steel, that's what you have."

"In your panties?" I asked.

"Sure, sweetie. It was thrilling; I felt like a drug smuggler."

"Well, lucky you," Carmen Elvira complained. "The last time I went to Colombia, when I came back they made me take off my panties. I was furious."

"That's right. You wrote that marvelous column about it. It created an international uproar, Sammy. It was reprinted in two Colombian newspapers."

"That's the power of the press for you," Carmen Elvira said solemnly, looking at me.

"What's *guascas*?" I asked. It seemed to me that I was at least two steps behind in the conversation, but since I had never heard of this herb or spice or whatever it was, I had to ask.

Olga had returned from the kitchen, and was setting a tray with drinks on the table. "What's that, honey?" she asked, handing me my Coke.

"*Guascas*," said Carmen Elvira.

I realized that as the culinary expert of the group, it was up to Olga to explain the mystery. "*Guascas*," she repeated, as she distributed the drinks. With an air of authority, she sat down and smoothed her dress. "In pre-Colombian times, the Indians used it as an aphrodisiac. It's rare because it only grows in the *paramo*. I, for one, think that if we could cultivate and export it commercially, Western cuisine as we know it would be revolutionized overnight."

"I'll be damned," I said.

Carmen Elvira said, "Sammy, you're such a gentleman. Lucy is so lucky to have a son who appreciates our national dishes." Then, making a tragic face, she confessed, "My children only eat hamburgers and pizza."

"Mine too," Irma said. "I don't know what I did wrong."

Olga said, "I cook my *arepas, frijoles*, and *sobrebarriga*, and all the things I love to eat. If they don't like it, then they can go eat at McDonald's. I cook to please myself; I'm not their servant."

"Right on," Irma cheered, making a fist.

"The last time I was in Colombia, everyone was eating hamburgers and pizza," I said. "Though Chinese takeout hadn't gotten there yet," I added.

"You were always so special," Carmen Elvira said to me. "From the time you were a boy you were so different from all the other children. That must be your poetic nature. You know, I used to say to my husband, 'If God had blessed me with a son, instead of five daughters, I wish he had been like Sammy.'"

I felt my face flush. "Thank you," I said.

"You have changed so much," Olga reminisced. "Irma," she said seriously, "you should have seen what huge ears he had when he was a boy."

"His ears look fine to me," Irma said in her curt, martinet manner.

"That's because you didn't know him back then. I have a picture of Sammy that now is of historic importance. Remind me to show it to you some day. His ears were not to be believed.

I had finished my *pastel* and was feeling terribly uncomfortable.

"Here, honey, have another one," Olga said.

"Thank you, very much. Not now." Seeing how disappointed she looked, I added, "Maybe later."

She said, "I promised Lucy I'd send her a couple of *pasteles* with you."

"She'll be so happy. She loves your *pasteles*. And I do too, but I had breakfast just a couple of hours ago. Maybe I'll take mine to Manhattan and have them later in the week."

"They taste better a few days later. Just freeze it, and when you want to eat it, warm it up in a *bano de Maria*."

Carmen Elvira asked, "Do you cook all your meals?"

I noted that, as the gossip columnist, Carmen Elvira mainly asked questions. "Yes," I informed her, "though not much in the summer; it gets too hot in the kitchen."

Olga said, "He'll make such a perfect husband for Claudia."

The other women nodded in agreement; they had finished their *pasteles*.

Olga said to Irma, "*Mijita*, will you help me clear the table and bring dessert? Then we can discuss the details of Sammy's induction over coffee and a cordial."

I watched Olga and Irma clear the table and disappear in the direction of the kitchen. I'd just set down my napkin when I noticed Carmen Elvira reaching for her handbag and pulling out a small tape recorder. I lit another cigarette.

"Testing, testing. One, two, three," she spoke into the contraption. "Sammy," Carmen Elvira said, winking at me, crossing her legs and exposing her knees, "why don't you come over here and sit next to me?"

Thinking she was about to make a pass at me, I said, "What? You want to interview me?"

"Yes, honey. I'm going to ask you a few questions for *Colombian Queens*," she explained, smiling.

"You know, Carmen Elvira, maybe this is not such a good time. I mean," I said, looking toward the kitchen door, "Irma and Olga will be coming back any minute."

"No, honey. They won't. They're doing the dishes and getting dessert ready while I interview you."

I realized I had been set up and that, as the guest of honor, it would be rude to decline the interview.

She interpreted my silence as acquiescence. "Here," she said pouring another *aguardiente* and handing me the little glass. "This will loosen you up."

I downed the *aguardiente*.

Patting the sofa, she said, "Come over here, Sammy. I'm not going to bite you. We'll just chat like two good old friends."

I sat next to her, feeling my forehead break into a sweat. "What kind of interview is this?"

She laughed. "You look as if you were facing a firing squad. Lighten up, honey. I'm just going to ask you a couple of questions, okay?"

"Okay." I put out my cigarette and lit another one.

"Ready?"

I nodded.

"We're here today with the award-winning poet Santiago Martinez Ardila, whose first book of poems *Lirio del Alba* (which, by the way, remains his only published title) will be remembered fondly by many poetry lovers, I'm sure. Today, however, we'll be talking to Santiago about other matters. Santiago, who has a Ph.D. in Medieval Studies from Queens College, and is a resident of Times Square, Manhattan, has announced today his plans to marry Claudia Urrutia."

"Wait a minute," I protested.

"Not now, honey," Carmen Elvira cut me off. "Claudia Urrutia, the import/export heiress of Barranquilla, Colombia; Jackson Heights, Queens; Miami, Florida; and Monte Carlo. Our Claudia, who trained in architecture at Yale, is also a great beauty and an accomplished..." Here Carmen Elvira looked lost. She motioned with her hand in front of my mouth, coaxing me to produce the word she wanted.

"Athlete," I ventured, remembering Claudia's fondness for motorcycles.

"Athlete. Yes. Athlete. Now, Santiago," she went on, pushing the machine against my nose, "tell us how you and Claudia met."

"This is preposterous. I'm not marrying Claudia Urrutia."

Carmen Elvira turned off the machine. She glared at me for

a second and then broke into a big, fake smile. Her thin scarlet lips stretched taut over her big white teeth. "You're such a naughty boy, Sammy. It's a well-known fact in the Colombian community that you and Claudia are tying the knot very soon. Both your mother and Claudia's have confirmed the news. I understand how you want to protect your privacy, but honey, you're our foremost poet in the United States and this is news to our readers."

She must have thought that by flattering me I would simply acquiesce as I had, after all, been doing all afternoon. Making an effort not to blow up (my mother would never have forgiven me if I offended her friends), I said, "Look, Carmen Elvira, I have no plans to get married at the moment.... But when I do, your readers will be the first to know. I promise. Cross my heart. Okay?"

Ignoring my speech, Carmen Elvira said, "Okay, Sammy. Don't you fret about it. I will fill out the details of the wedding. I know men don't like to talk about this sort of thing." Then she pushed the ON button and said, "Today, Santiago Martinez Ardila has been inducted as a member of The Colombian Parnassus, thus becoming the first male member of our society. Santiago, dear, we know that for the past ten years you've been working on a book of poems about Christopher Columbus."

"An epic poem, to be precise."

"We understand that this great...masterpiece, which will add glory to our national poetry, is almost finished. Is that so?"

"Not at all."

Totally unperturbed, she asked, "And is it in free verse or in rhyme?"

"Free verse, of course. I'm a modern poet."

"How innovative," Carmen Elvira said. "How avant-garde. May I ask what drew you to the subject of the Admiral of the Seven Seas?"

This was the first legitimate question she had asked. How-

-ever, I had been writing the poem for such a long time that I could no longer remember why I had been drawn to Columbus originally.

"Could it have been his liaison with Queen Isabella?" Carmen Elvira (quick to dish everyone) came to my rescue.

"Certainly not."

She looked disappointed. "What is your opinion about the recent theory that Columbus was a woman?"

My jaw must have fallen open. In any case, Carmen Elvira did not wait for an answer. "We hope this long-awaited poem will be finished by 1992, the 500th anniversary of the discovery of America. We wish you great luck, both with it and your forthcoming marriage." She turned off the machine and thanked me for the interview.

I was about to let her have a piece of my mind, when Olga and Irma burst into the room with dessert. Olga carried a tray with cheese, *obleas*, guava paste, stuffed figs and *arequipe*, and Irma the *tinto* service. While the sweets were being served on the saucers, I noticed Olga stealing glances at Carmen Elvira as if to find out how the interview had turned out. But the latter pretended to fuss with her glasses, ignoring Olga. We tasted the sweets in silence, making sounds of approval and sipping our *tintos*.

Olga said, "Tell us, Sammy, how does it feel to be a brand new member of The Parnassus? It's been so many years since I became a member. But I remember how honored I felt. I envy the way you feel right now."

"Yes," I said politely. "And what do I have to do now?"

"It's very simple," Carmen Elvira informed me. "We meet on the last Saturday of every month, except during August. It is suggested that all members attend the monthly meeting. Also, there are no dues or annual fees."

"Oh, good," I said, relieved.

"But to become a member there is a three hundred fifty dollar fee. Considering that it covers lifetime membership, it's a steal."

They offered me the perfect excuse, and I jumped at it. "I'm very honored to have been invited to join The Parnassus, but the truth is, I'm not solvent at the moment and three hundred fifty bucks is a lot of money for me. So maybe next year."

"Don't worry about it, sweetie," Olga reassured me. "Lucy was well aware of this and she has offered to take care of it."

"What? My mother is going to pay the fee?" I asked in disbelief, considering the many occasions she had denied me loans for small amounts.

"That's a mother's love for you, Sammy," Olga said.

"Treasure your mother while she's alive, and make her happy," Irma said. "I didn't know how lucky I was while my mom was alive, and I'll never get over it now."

"You just don't know how much you'll miss her when she's gone," Carmen Elvira prophesized.

"Let me explain a bit more in depth what is required to be a member," Olga said, taking a dainty bite of cheese and then licking her fingers. "A new member has to do some group service to join in."

"What kind of service?"

Carmen Elvira said, "Since you're a translator—"

"An interpreter," I corrected her.

"Well, it's the same thing, honey, isn't it?"

"Absolutely not," I said, setting down my saucer and glaring at her.

"It's almost the same thing," Olga said, "so why quibble?"

"Anyway," Carmen Elvira went on, "since you're an interpreter, we thought you'd be perfect for this. As you know, we are all poets. Not award-winning poets like you, but nonetheless serious poets."

"I've been writing poetry since I was seven," Olga said.

Carmen Elvira stared at me, waiting for me to certify their bona fides. "I didn't start quite that early," I said.

"In any case, I'm sure you've read our poems in *Colombian Queens*. We all publish quite regularly."

"Oh yes," I lied. I had glanced at their gibberish on occasion to please my mother.

"I especially recommend this issue's selection," Olga said. "Carmen Elvira wrote the loveliest poem about the volcano disaster in Manizales, you remember? It's unbearably moving; Homeric in its ambition. If you encourage her, maybe Carmen Elvira will be gracious enough to recite it for you now."

Carmen Elvira was smiling and fluttering her hands and eyelids, so I hastened to say, "Thank you very much, but I promise you I'll read it tonight, in bed. That's how I read poetry. I never go to readings; I don't like people reading at me."

"How peculiar," Irma said.

"How un-Colombian," Olga added.

"What is it that you want me to translate?" I asked.

"Sammy, we've decided to go legit and to publish our poems in a collection," Olga said, clasping her hands. "And we've chosen you to translate them into English since you're such a talented poet, from our own country, and perfectly bilingual."

"What?" I croaked.

"And we'd love it if you could write an introduction. It doesn't have to be very long. We leave it entirely up to you, as long as it's written from the heart."

"But I've never translated any poetry into English. I think you've got the wrong guy for this project," I stammered.

"Your modesty is appealing," Olga squealed flirtatiously, like a superannuated Lolita. "You'll do beautifully. We already have the title for you: *Muses of Queens*. Do you like it?"

"Can I have an *aguardiente*?" was my response.

"Of course, honey. You're right; this calls for a toast."

Once more we chugged down our drinks, toasting to poetry. It occurred to me that by joining the toast I was accepting their proposition just as I had already tacitly confirmed my engagement to Claudia. "Let me explain something," I said. "I have to think about this. I mean, as much as I'd like to do it, I don't know if I have the time right now."

"We understand, don't we, girls?" Carmen Elvira said.

"Take your time," added Olga.

"There's absolutely no hurry," Irma said. "What with your wedding and everything else, we don't want to put any extra pressure on you. When we meet again in September, we can discuss the details."

"What's more," Olga intervened, "we'd really love to pay you, but we have children going to college, so we live pretty close to what we make."

"We can't pay you in cash, that's true. But we have something much more valuable to offer you."

Shuddering, I asked, "Like what?"

"Power," she said. "That's right, honey, power! As a new member of The Parnassus you automatically become a contributing editor to *Colombian Queens*. You are aware of what that means, aren't you?"

"No. What does it mean?"

"It means you can reach one million compatriots in the greater New York area. Our magazine reaches practically every member of this community. Think of the great audience you'll have for your poetry and your ideas."

"Did you know that the future of the next presidential election in Colombia is in our hands?" Olga giggled.

"No kidding!"

"We're a political force; we're a crucial element in the next presidential election. The candidates we endorse will receive about one hundred thousand votes, which is almost as many votes as there will be cast in all Colombia. You know our people are abstentionists, and only government employees go to the polls."

"Gee whiz," I said, genuinely impressed by their reasoning, though doubtful of their statistics.

Carmen Elvira said, "Your vote is of historical significance, Sammy."

"But I've never voted."

"Why not?" asked Olga, looking concerned.

"I don't know very much about Colombian politics."

She sighed with obvious relief. "That's all right. I thought it was something worse. Well, sweetie, this is your chance to learn. You couldn't ask for better teachers. We're all seasoned political campaigners."

"Do you always vote?" I asked stupidly.

"I can't vote," Carmen Elvira stated somberly.

This was interesting. "Why not?"

"She's an American citizen," Irma said.

"So are you," Carmen Elvira counterattacked angrily. "And you too, Olga."

"I don't deny it, *mijita*," a dejected Olga corroborated. "But I'm a Colombian at heart and will die Colombian."

"Me too," Carmen Elvira said, full of patriotic fervor. I just did it so that my children could have a better chance in this country."

"I was practically forced to do it," Olga said, "In my ignorance, I thought I had to become a citizen in order to keep my federal job."

"Save your speeches; this is not the Inquisition," Carmen Elvira said cattily. "We did it, and that's that. Period."

To cheer them up, I said, "My mother is an American citizen, too."

"Don't you ever become one," Carmen Elvira ordered me. "It would be disgraceful, a real tragedy of the first magnitude if our leading poet in the States became an American."

"I wonder if Garcia Marquez is a Mexican," Olga pondered. "I think I read it somewhere that he became a Mexican citizen a few years ago."

"I don't believe it for a second," snapped Carmen Elvira, slapping her knee. "Gabo would never do that. He'd never betray his country; he's one hundred fifty percent Colombian."

"But he's lived in Mexico for thirty years," Olga insisted.

"So what?"

"His children were born in Mexico," Olga expatiated.

"I don't care what the *National Enquirer* prints," Carmen Elvira scoffed, chugging down another *aguardiente*. Her speech was becoming slurred. "Gabo and Colombia will always be one, indivisible."

"Yes," Irma seconded her. "Like the Father, the Son, and the Holy Ghost."

The theological turn of the conversation warned me it was time to split. "I got to go," I said. "I have to go visit a friend."

Always the gossip, Carmen Elvira inquired, "Claudia?"

"No, my friend Bobby."

"Bobby Castro? Is it true he has AIDS?"

I stood up. "Yes, he's dying. Thank you for the delicious lunch. It was ... nice to see you all," I said. Now that I was standing, I realized the *aguardiente* had gone to my head; my feet were wobbly, and the ladies and the room swam in front of my eyes. "And I'm really ... pleased to be a member of The Parnassus."

"Wait," Olga said. "I promised Lucy a couple of *pasteles.*"

Irma said, "Send her some figs. They're really fresh. My cousin brought them from Bogota yesterday. These are Buga figs, Sammy. Be sure to tell that to your mother; she adores Buga figs. Actually, take all of them. I have plenty more at home," she finished magnanimously.

Minutes later, after another *aguardiente* for the road, and carrying a supermarket bag filled with Colombian delicacies, I staggered into the afternoon sun.

Yala Korwin
IMMIGRANT'S LAMENT

Here they say: We're friends, call.
When I do, they don't remember
my name.
In the old country, they say:
You're welcome, come in.

Here they ask: How are you?
Before I can tell, they hurry
away.
There, when they don't ask, I know
they don't want to know.

Whenever I talk: Where
are you from? From the world's center,
I say.
They don't believe me. Here is
the center, they say.

My Polish Mom fed me
too much love, worries, and cabbage
with peas.
There, no one needed a shrink;
mother was just Mom.

Now, a mother myself,
I'm never sure: How much to give?
How little?
Whatever I choose, I'll be
lost in translation.

AMERICA! AMERICA!

When the visa arrived
the world somersaulted
all boundaries burst
a million suns rose
and a million bells rang
resounding in my ears:
America! America!

That morning on the deck
of the shore-nearing liner
early haze lifted
unveiling the lone lady
of the green torch and crown
on her tiny island
beaten by foaming breakers.

In the New York port pounded
by multitudes of feet
where no one waited
late sun hid
behind skyscrapers
offering long shadows
like roses with tall stems.

David Low
WINTERBLOSSOM GARDEN

I have no photographs of my father. One hot Saturday in June, my camera slung over my shoulder, I take the subway from Greenwich Village to Chinatown. I switch to the M local which becomes an elevated train after it crosses the Williamsburg Bridge. I am going to Ridgewood, Queens, where I spent my childhood. I sit in a car that is almost empty; I feel the loud rumble of the whole train through the hard seat. Someday, I think, wiping the sweat from my face, they'll tear this el down, as they've torn down the others.

I get off at Fresh Pond Road and walk the five blocks from the station to my parents' restaurant. At the back of the store in the kitchen, I find my father packing an order: white cartons of food fit neatly into a brown paper bag. As the workers chatter in Cantonese, I smell the food cooking: spare ribs, chicken lo mein, sweet and pungent pork, won ton soup. My father, who has just turned seventy-three, wears a wrinkled white short-sleeve shirt and a cheap maroon tie, even in this weather. He dabs his face with a handkerchief.

"Do you need money?" he asks in Chinese, as he takes the order to the front of the store. I notice that he walks slower than usual. Not that his walk is ever very fast; he usually walks with quiet assurance, a man who knows who he is and where he is going. Other people will just have to wait until he gets there.

"Not this time," I answer in English. I laugh. I haven't borrowed money from him in years but he still asks. My father and I have almost always spoken different languages.

"I want to take your picture, Dad."

"Not now, too busy." He hands the customer the order and rings the cash register.

"It will only take a minute."

He stands reluctantly beneath the green awning in front of the store, next to the gold-painted letters on the window:

WINTERBLOSSOM GARDEN
CHINESE-AMERICAN RESTAURANT
WE SERVE THE FINEST FOOD
I look through the camera viewfinder.

"Smile," I say.

Instead my father holds his left hand with the crooked pinky on his stomach. I have often wondered about that pinky; is it a souvenir of some street fight in his youth? He wears a jade ring on his index finger. His hair, streaked with gray, is greased down as usual; his face looks a little pale. Most of the day, he remains at the restaurant. I snap the shutter.

"Go see your mother," he says slowly in English.

According to my mother, in 1929 my father entered this country illegally by jumping off the boat as it neared Ellis Island and swimming to Hoboken, New Jersey; there he managed to board a train to New York, even though he knew no English and had not one American cent in his pockets. Whether or not the story is true, I like to imagine my father hiding in the washroom on the train, dripping wet with fatigue and feeling triumphant. Now he was in America, where anything could happen. He found a job scooping ice cream at a dance hall in Chinatown. My mother claims that before he married her, he liked to gamble his nights away and drink with scandalous women. After two years in this country, he opened his restaurant with money he had borrowed from friends in Chinatown who already ran their own businesses. My father chose Ridgewood for the store's location because he mistook the community's name for "Richwood." In such a lucky place, he told my mother, his restaurant was sure to succeed.

When I was growing up, my parents spent most of their days in Winterblossom Garden. Before going home after school, I would stop at the restaurant. The walls then were a hideous pale green with red numbers painted in Chinese characters and Roman numerals above the side booths. In days of warm weather huge fans whirred from the ceiling. My mother would

sit at a table in the back where she would make egg rolls. She
began by placing generous handfuls of meat-and-cabbage filling on squares of thin white dough. Then she delicately folded up each piece of dough, checking to make sure the filling
was totally sealed inside, like a mummy wrapped in bandages.
Finally, with a small brush she spread beaten eggs on the outside of each white roll. As I watched her steadily produce a
tray of these uncooked creations, she never asked me about
school; she was more concerned that my shirt was sticking out
of my pants or that my hair was disheveled.

"Are you hungry?" my mother would ask in English. Although my parents had agreed to speak only Chinese in my
presence, she often broke this rule when my father wasn't in
the same room. Whether I wanted to eat or not, I was sent into the kitchen where my father would repeat my mother's
question. Then without waiting for an answer, he would prepare for me a bowl of beef with snow peas or a small portion
of steamed fish. My parents assumed that as long as I ate well,
everything in my life would be fine. If I said "Hello" or "Thank
you" in Chinese, I was allowed to choose whatever dish I liked;
often I ordered a hot turkey sandwich. I liked the taste of
burnt rice soaked in tea.

I would wait an hour or so for my mother to walk home
with me. During that time, I would go to the front of the store,
put a dime in the jukebox and press the buttons for a currently popular song. It might be D3: "Bye Bye, Love." Then I
would lean on the back of the bench where customers waited
for take-outs; I would stare out the large window that faced
the street. The world outside seemed vast, hostile and often
sad.

Across the way, I could see Rosa's Italian Bakery, the Western Union office and Von Ronn's soda fountain. Why didn't
we live in Chinatown? I wondered. Or San Francisco? In a
neighborhood that was predominantly German, I had no Chinese friends. No matter how many bottles of Coca Cola I
drank, I would still be different from the others. They were

fond of calling me "Skinny Chink" when I won games of stoop ball. I wanted to have blond curly hair and blue eyes; I didn't understand why my father didn't have a ranch like the rugged cowboys on television.

Now Winterblossom Garden has wood-paneling on the walls, formica tables and aluminum Roman numerals over the mock-leather booths. Several years ago, when the ceiling was lowered, the whirring fans were removed; a huge air-conditioning unit was installed. The jukebox has been replaced by Muzak. My mother no longer makes the egg rolls; my father hires enough help to do that.

Some things remain the same. My father has made few changes in the menu, except for the prices; the steady customers know they can always have the combination plates. In a glass case near the cash register, cardboard boxes overflow with bags of fortune cookies and almond candies that my father gives away free to children. The first dollar bill my parents ever made hangs framed on the wall above the register. Next to that dollar, a picture of my parents taken twenty years ago recalls a time when they were raising four children at once, paying mortgages and putting in the bank every cent that didn't go toward bills. Although it was a hard time for them, my mother's face is radiant, as if she has just won the top prize at a beauty pageant; she wears a flower-print dress with a large white collar. My father has on a suit with wide lapels that was tailored in Chinatown; he is smiling a rare smile.

My parents have a small brick house set apart from the other buildings on the block. Most of their neighbors have lived in Ridgewood all their lives. As I ring the bell and wait for my mother to answer, I notice that the maple tree in front of the house has died. All that is left is a gray ghost; bare branches lie in the gutter. If I took a picture of this tree, I think, the printed image would resemble a negative.

"The gas man killed it when they tore up the street," my mother says. She watches television as she lies back on the gold sofa like a queen, her head resting against a pillow. A documentary about wildlife in Africa is on the screen; gazelles dance across a dusty plain. My mother likes soap operas but they aren't shown on weekends. In the evenings she will watch almost anything except news specials and police melodramas.

"Why don't you get a new tree planted?"

"We would have to get a permit," she answers. "The sidewalk belongs to the city. Then we would have to pay for the tree."

"It would be worth it," I say. "Doesn't it bother you, seeing a dead tree everyday? You should find someone to cut it down."

My mother does not answer. She has fallen asleep. These days she can doze off almost as soon as her head touches the pillow. Six years ago she had a nervous breakdown. When she came home from the hospital she needed to take naps in the afternoon. Soon the naps became a permanent refuge, a way to forget her loneliness for an hour or two. She no longer needed to work in the store. Three of her children were married. I was away at art school and planned to live on my own when I graduated.

"I have never felt at home in America," my mother once told me.

Now as she lies there, I wonder if she is dreaming. I would like her to tell me her darkest dream. Although we speak the same language, there has always been an ocean between us. She does not wish to know what I think alone at night, what I see of the world with my camera.

My mother pours two cups of tea from the porcelain teapot that has always been in its wicker basket on the kitchen table. On the sides of the teapot, a maiden dressed in a jade-green gown visits a bearded emperor at his palace near the sky. The maiden waves a vermillion fan.

"I bet you still don't know how to cook," my mother says. She places a plate of steamed roast pork buns before me.

"Mom, I'm not hungry."

"If you don't eat more, you will get sick."

I take a bun from the plate but it is too hot. My mother hands me a napkin so I can put the bun down. Then she peels a banana in front of me.

"I'm not obsessed with food like you," I say.

"What's wrong with eating?"

She looks at me as she takes a big bite of the banana.

"I'm going to have a photography show at the end of the summer."

"Are you still taking pictures of old buildings falling down? How ugly! Why don't you take happier pictures?"

"I thought you would want to come," I answer. "It's not easy to get a gallery."

"If you were married," she says, her voice becoming unusually soft, "you would take better pictures. You would be happy."

"I don't know what you mean. Why do you think getting married will make me happy?"

My mother looks at me as if I have spoken in Serbo-Croatian. She always gives me this look when I say something she does not want to hear. She finishes the banana; then she puts the plate of food away. Soon she stands at the sink, turns on the hot water and washes dishes. My mother learned long ago that silence has a power of its own.

She takes out a blue cookie tin from the dining room cabinet. Inside this tin, my mother keeps her favorite photographs. Whenever I am ready to leave, she brings it to the living room and opens it on the coffee table. She knows I cannot resist looking at these pictures again; I will sit down next to her on the sofa for at least another hour. Besides the portraits of the family, my mother has images of people I have never met: her father who owned a poultry store on Pell Street and didn't get a chance to return to China before he died; my father's younger sister who still runs a pharmacy in Rio de Janeiro (she sends the family an annual supply of cough drops); my mother's cousin, Kay who died at thirty, a year after she came to New York from Hong Kong. Although my mother has a story to tell for each photograph, she refuses to speak about Kay, as if the mere mention of her name will bring back her ghost to haunt us all.

My mother always manages to find a picture I have not seen before; suddenly I discover I have a relative who is a mortician in Vancouver. I pick up a portrait of Uncle Lao-Hu, a silver-haired man with a goatee who owned a curio shop on Mott Street until he retired last year and moved to Hawaii. In a color print, he stands in the doorway of his store, holding a bamboo Moon Man in front of him, as if it were a bowling trophy. The statue, which is actually two feet tall, has a staff in its left hand, while its right palm balances a peach, a sign of long life. The top of the Moon Man's head protrudes in the shape of an eggplant; my mother believes that such a head contains an endless wealth of wisdom.

"Your Uncle Lao-Hu is a wise man, too," my mother says, "except when he's in love. When he still owned the store, he fell in love with his women customers all the time. He was always losing money because he gave away his merchandise to any woman who smiled at him."

I see my uncle's generous arms full of gifts: a silver Buddha, an ivory dragon, a pair of emerald chopsticks.

"These women confused him," she adds. "That's what happens when a Chinese man doesn't get married."

My mother shakes her head and sighs.

"In his last letter, Lao-Hu invited me to visit him in Honolulu. Your father refuses to leave the store."

"Why don't you go anyway?"

"I can't leave your father alone." She stares at the pictures scattered on the coffee table.

"Mom, why don't you do something for yourself? I thought you were going to start taking English lessons."

"Your father thinks it would be a waste of time."

While my mother puts the cookie tin away, I stand up to

stretch my legs. I gaze at a photograph that hangs on the wall
above my parents' wedding picture. My mother was matched
to my father; she claims that if her own father had been able
to repay the money that Dad spent to bring her to America,
she might never have married him at all. In the wedding picture she wears a stunned expression. She is dressed in a luminous gown of ruffles and lace; the train spirals at her feet. As
she clutches a bouquet tightly against her stomach, she might
be asking, "What am I doing? Who is this man?" My father's
face is thinner than it is now. His tuxedo is too small for him;
the flower in his lapel droops. He hides his hand with the
crooked pinky behind his back.

I have never been sure if my parents really love each other.
I have only seen them kiss at their children's weddings. They
never touch each other in public. When I was little, I often
thought they went to sleep in the clothes they wore to work.

Before I leave, my mother asks me to take her picture. Unlike my father she likes to pose for photographs as much as
possible. When her children still lived at home, she would leave
snapshots of herself all around the house; we could not forget
her, no matter how hard we tried.

She changes her blouse, combs her hair and redoes her eye-
brows. Then I follow her out the back door into the garden
where she kneels down next to the rose bush. She touches one
of the yellow roses.

"Why don't you sit on the front steps?" I ask, as I peer
through the viewfinder. "It will be more natural."

"No," she says firmly. "Take the picture now."

She smiles without opening her mouth. I see for the first
time that she has put on a pair of dangling gold earrings. Her
face has grown round as the moon with the years. She has developed wrinkles under the eyes, but like my father, she hardly shows her age. For the past ten years, she has been fifty-one.
Everyone needs a fantasy to help them stay alive: my mother
believes she is perpetually beautiful, even if my father has not

complimented her in years.

After I snap the shutter, she plucks a rose.

As we enter the kitchen through the back door, I can hear my father's voice from the next room.

"Who's he talking to?" I ask.

"He's talking to the goldfish," she answers. "I have to live with this man."

My father walks in, carrying a tiny can of fish food.

"You want a girlfriend?" he asks out of nowhere. "My friend has a nice daughter. She knows how to cook Chinese food."

"Dad, she sounds perfect for you."

"She likes to stay home," my mother adds. "She went to college and reads books like you."

"I'll see you next year," I say.

That evening in the darkroom at my apartment, I develop and print my parents' portraits. I hang the pictures side by side to dry on a clothesline in the bathroom. As I feel my parents' eyes staring at me, I turn away. Their faces look unfamiliar in the fluorescent light.

II

At the beginning of July my mother calls me at work.

"Do you think you can take off next Monday morning?" she asks.

"Why?"

"Your father has to go to the hospital for some tests. He looks awful."

We sit in the back of a taxi on the way to a hospital in Forest Hills. I am sandwiched between my mother and father. The skin of my father's face is pale yellow. During the past few weeks he has lost fifteen pounds; his wrinkled suit is baggy around the waist. My mother sleeps with her head tilted to one side until the taxi hits a bump on the road. She wakes up startled, as if afraid she has missed a stop on the train.

"Don't worry," my father says weakly. He squints as he turns his head toward the window. "The doctors will give me pills. Everything will be fine."

"Don't say anything," my mother says. "Too much talk will bring bad luck."

My father takes two crumpled dollar bills from his jacket and places them in my hand.

"For the movies," he says. I smile, without mentioning it costs more to go to a film these days.

My mother opens her handbag and takes out a compact. She has forgotten to put on her lipstick.

The hospital waiting room has beige walls. My mother and I follow my father as he makes his way slowly to a row of seats near an open window.

"Fresh air is important," he used to remind me on a sunny day when I would read a book in bed. Now after we sit down, he keeps quiet. I hear the sound of plates clattering from the coffee shop in the next room.

"Does anyone want some breakfast?" I ask.

"Your father can't eat anything before the tests," my mother warns.

"What about you?"

"I'm not hungry," she says.

My father reaches over to take my hand in his. He considers my palm.

"Very, very lucky," he says. "You will have lots of money."

I laugh. "You've been saying that ever since I was born."

He puts on his glasses crookedly and touches a curved line near the top of my palm.

"Be patient," he says.

My mother rises suddenly.

"Why are they making us wait so long? Do you think they forgot us?"

While she walks over to speak to a nurse at the reception

desk, my father leans toward me.

"Remember to take care of your mother."

The doctors discover that my father has stomach cancer. They decide to operate immediately. According to them, he has already lost so much blood that it is a miracle he is still alive.

The week of my father's operation, I sleep at my parents' house. My mother has kept my bedroom on the second floor the way it was before I moved out. A square room, it gets the afternoon light. Dust covers the top of my old bookcase. The first night I stay over I find a pinhole camera on a shelf in the closet; I made it when I was twelve, from a cylindrical Quaker Oats box. When I lie back on the yellow comforter that covers my bed, I see the crack in the ceiling that I once called the Yangtze River, the highway for tea merchants and vagabonds.

At night I help my mother close the restaurant. I do what she and my father have done together for the past forty-three years. At ten o'clock I turn off the illuminated white sign above the front entrance. After all the customers leave and the last waiter says goodbye, I lock the front door and flip over the sign that says "Closed." Then I shut off the radio and the back lights. While I refill the glass case with bottles of duck sauce and packs of cigarettes, my mother empties the cash register. She puts all the money in white cartons and packs them in brown paper bags. My father thought up that idea long ago.

In the past when they have walked the three blocks home, they have given the appearance of carrying bags of food. The one time my father was attacked by three teenagers, my mother was sick in bed. My father scared the kids off by pretending he knew kung fu. When he got home, he showed me his swollen left hand and smiled.

"Don't tell your mother."

On the second night we walk home together, my mother says:

"I could never run the restaurant alone. I would have to sell it. I have four children and no one wants it."

I say nothing, unwilling to start an argument.

Later my mother and I eat jello in the kitchen. A cool breeze blows through the window.

"Maybe I will sleep tonight," my mother says. She walks out to the back porch to sit on one of the two folding chairs. My bedroom is right above the porch; as a child I used to hear my parents talking late into the night, their paper fans rustling.

After reading a while in the living room, I go upstairs to take a shower. When I am finished, I hear my mother calling my name from downstairs.

I find her dressed in her bathrobe, opening the dining room cabinet.

"Someone has stolen the money," she says. She walks nervously into the living room and looks under the lamp table.

"What are you talking about?" I ask.

"Maybe we should call the police," she suggests. "I can't find the money we brought home tonight."

She starts to pick up the phone.

"Wait. Have you checked everywhere? Where do you usually put it?"

"I thought I locked it in your father's closet but it isn't there."

"I'll look around," I say. "Why don't you go back to sleep?"

She lies back on the sofa.

"How can I sleep?" she asks. "I told your father a long time ago to sell the restaurant but he wouldn't listen."

I search the first floor. I look in the shoe closet, behind the television, underneath the dining room table, in the clothes hamper. Finally after examining all the kitchen cupboards without any luck, I open the refrigerator to take out something to drink. The three cartons of money are on the second shelf, next to the mayonnaise and the strawberry jam.

When I bring the cartons to the living room, my mother sits up on the sofa, amazed.

"Well," she says, "how did they ever get *there*?"

She opens one of them. The crisp dollar bills inside are cold as ice.

The next day I talk on the telephone to my father's physician. He informs me that the doctors have succeeded in removing the malignancy before it has spread. My father will remain in intensive care for at least a week.

In the kitchen my mother irons a tablecloth.

"The doctors are impressed by Dad's willpower, considering his age," I tell her.

"A fortune teller on East Broadway told him that he will live to be a hundred," she says.

That night I dream that I am standing at the entrance to Winterblossom Garden. A taxi stops in front of the store. My father jumps out, dressed in a bathrobe and slippers.

"I'm almost better," he tells me. "I want to see how the business is doing without me."

In a month he is ready to come home. My sister Elizabeth, the oldest child, picks him up at the hospital. At the house the whole family waits for him.

When Elizabeth's car arrives my mother and I are already standing on the front steps. My sister walks around the car to open my father's door. He cannot get out by himself. My sister offers him a hand but as he reaches out to grab it, he misses and falls back in his seat.

Finally my sister helps him stand up, his back a little stooped. While my mother remains on the steps, I run to give a hand.

My father does not fight our help. His skin is dry and pale but no longer yellow. As he walks forward, staring at his feet, I feel his whole body shaking against mine. Only now, as he leans his weight on my arm, do I begin to understand how easily he might have died. He seems light as a sparrow.

When we reach the front steps, my father raises his head to look at my mother. She stares at him a minute, then turns away to open the door. Soon my sister and I are leading him to the living room sofa, where we help him lie back. My mother has a pillow and a blanket ready. She sits down on the coffee table in front of him. I watch them hold each other's hands.

III

At the beginning of September my photography exhibit opens at a cooperative gallery on West 13th Street. I have chosen to hang only a dozen pictures, not much to show for ten years of work. About sixty people come to the opening, more than I expected; I watch them from a corner of the room, now and then overhearing a conversation I would like to ignore.

After an hour I decide I have stayed too long. As I walk around the gallery, hunting for a telephone, I see my parents across the room. My father calls out my name in Chinese; he has gained back all his weight and appears to be in better shape than many of the people around him. As I make my way toward my parents, I hear him talking loudly in bad English to a short young woman who stares at one of my portraits.

"That's my wife," he says. "If you like it, you should buy it."

"Maybe I will," the young woman says. She points to another photograph. "Isn't that you?"

My father laughs. "No, that's my brother."

My mother hands me a brown paper bag.

"Leftover from dinner," she tells me. "You didn't tell me you were going to show my picture. It's the best one in the show."

I take my parents for a personal tour.

"Who is that?" my father asks. He stops at a photograph of a naked woman covered from the waist down by a pile of leaves as she sits in the middle of a forest.

"She's a professional model," I lie.

"She needs to gain some weight," my mother says.

A few weeks after my show has closed, I have lunch with

my parents at the restaurant. After we finish our meal, my father walks into the kitchen to scoop ice cream for dessert. My mother opens her handbag. She takes out a worn manila envelope and hands it to me across the table.

"I found this in a box while I was cleaning the house," she says. "I want you to have it."

Inside the envelope, I find a portrait of my father, taken when he was still a young man. He does not smile but his eyes shine like wet black marbles. He wears a polka-dot tie; a plaid handkerchief hangs out of the front pocket of his suit jacket. My father has never cared about his clothes matching. Even when he was young, he liked to grease down his hair with Brilliantine.

"Your father's cousin was a doctor in Hong Kong," my mother tells me. "After my eighteenth birthday, he came to my parents' house and showed them this picture. He said your father would make the perfect husband because he was handsome and very smart. Grandma gave me the picture before I got on the boat to America."

"I'll have it framed right away."

My father returns with three dishes of chocolate ice cream balanced on a silver tray.

"You want to work here?" he asks me.

"Your father wants to sell the business next year," my mother says. "He feels too old to run a restaurant."

"I'd just lose money," I say. "Besides, Dad, you're not old."

He does not join us for dessert. Instead, he dips his napkin in a glass of water and starts to wipe the table. I watch his dish of ice cream melt.

When I am ready to leave, my parents walk me to the door.

"Next time, I'll take you uptown to see a movie," I say as we step outside.

"Radio City?" my father asks.

"They don't show movies there now," my mother reminds him.

"I'll cook dinner for you at my apartment."

My father laughs.

"We'll eat out," my mother suggests.

My parents wait in front of Winterblossom Garden until I reach the end of the block. I turn and wave. With her heels on, my mother is the same height as my father. She waves back for both of them. I would like to take their picture, but I forgot to bring my camera.

Susan Montez
BUENOS AIRES NOTEBOOK

1) Travel Agent Divertimento

Alone in Queens with horseradish
    divorced, roast beef for lunch,
I type: Dear John: I've had it
        with the glamour life,
        free travel, but no money,
        I quit, good
        Sincerely, Agent 20.
Radio, "Quiero Rock", Mookie in left field,
    the fan whirs: "Don't quit yet. There's someone
to meet on the 7:05 Buenos Aires to Iguazu!"
    a flight booked last month, a connection
        for a client, not for me.

*This client, Herr Baer, I'd had a crush on since processing his
visa for Argentina. According to his visa form, he was perfect
for me. Born in 1942, he was Swiss, divorced and living on
Joralemon Street. I wanted to marry him and move to
Brooklyn Heights, lounge with books, drink coffee at cafes
mid-day.*

*No that's not true. What I really wanted to do was stick Peter—
throw another husband in his face—but bigger bargaining
collateral this time.*

    No more flights, no more flying
feet on the clouds. Ahh, but Argentina!
    Perons, cafes, waterfalls, maybe
one last free ride before I'm wingless,
    grounded, a stone.
Drop off cat, bounce a few checks,
    tonight black sky, sapphire runway,
Astoria lights below.

Actually, I don't go anywhere unless I have to. As Matthew Arnold once said, "There's not a damn thing out there." Of course, it was different with Peter. Every three weeks I was on the 9 o'clock Lufthansa to Frankfurt or Pan Am to Dubrovnik (with a change in Zurich and stop in Zagreb).

Now I stay around the neighborhood, go out to Shea on the weekend, maybe to Brooklyn (not the Heights), or the Village.

2) Barado/Retrasado

Always the same. Now Buenos Aires,
    Aeroparque—across the road
the world's widest river, La Plata del Rio,
    winter palm trees. Inside passengers
are piled at the gate, flight delays, fog, rain,
    low ceilings in Iguazu.

This is bullshit, and I can't believe what I'm doing—retracing Herr Baer's itinerary. This Iguazu flight is where I thought the action was, but now the only action seems to be delays. See, according to Herr Baer, I made a mess of his South America trip. Liar, he messed it up himself by being an asshole with the Brasilian authorities. But I took advantage of his claim (since we hadn't met yet, and I was planning to marry him), called him up and said, "So sorry, let me take you to lunch."

I took him to the Algonquin, the Rose Room. He looked just like his picture. He also reminded me of Peter, or I pretended he did. Really I found his accent obnoxious where I'd found Peter's German one charming.

2 weeks later, I wrote him a note.
    Dear Herr Baer:
    I've had a crush on you since October.
    I thought you'd ask me out when we had

lunch. You should have, you'd like me.
I'd fetch you trifles and never leave you
at the mercy of wild beasts.

He ignored it. Paula said, "What'd you expect? He's Swiss. You
should have written the note to his father asking permission."

Out 85 bucks for lunch (there's no price tag on love, but there
is on fuck-ups), I thought, fuck Herr Baer. he's not my angel,
my angel's on the flight to Iguazu.

Maybe the flight will be cancelled. Maybe
 I'll skip the jungle, Niagara would have been
closer anyway,

I used to book German tourists to Niagara every Saturday.
That was when Peter was my client. At first, he was a dope,
flirting, then bugging me about cheap fares for his groups to
Miami—before we fell in love, before I knew he'd been living
with Ushi, a cross-eyed girl in a fox coat, for 17 years (refusing
to marry her), before he got transferred, before I got married,
before the day came when neither of us would be at 165 West
46th Street, me on the 9th floor, he on the 8th.

  but no—besides, there he is—
 jeans, white shirt, so young—
the one destined to this flight, the one
 I don't know, but will meet when
the fog lifts, wing flaps go down, rubber
 wheels bounce Iguazu runway.
I get up, go to the counter, order cafe solo.
 "No tengo cambio."
He follows. I look, he looks, nobody looks.
 I get out a book, if it were up to me
  all planes would be grounded.

I hate this flying around business. Travel restrictions, like
Communist countries had, are sensible. Loved ones stuck in
Queens by order of the government, there's an idea. OK, I
wouldn't have met Peter, but then, if I'd never met the love
of my life—what would I be missing?

3) Las Cataratas Del Iguazu

We meet on the plane (always the same),
    32,000 feet, I hang
over his seat. He's going on to Sao Paolo,
    making his change, but we exchange
names, numbers, Alberto. Alberto, citizen
    of Colombia but lives in Bethesda. We part
at passports like we should kiss, but don't.

At Frankfurt Airport, Peter'd say, "We can't smooz here—not
with all my colleagues around." But we smoozed anyway.
Serious smooz. Hollywood. He must have been looking to get
caught. The only place he ever refused me (the last place we'd
get caught) was at the War Memorial for Yugoslav Partisans.
It wasn't polite with all the Czechs paying homage to a system
that didn't work.

I don't dawdle—a rush to go
    nowhere. Damp green jungle,
taxis, tour buses, guides with whistles,
    "Over here, please. People, people!"
outside the glass terminal.

Peter started in the travel business as a guide in Constanta,
Roumania. Except for 7 years in New York, he was always
getting assigned to countries "under the pressure". He'd call
from Yugoslavia and say, "It's not here, and the Communists
are bugging me."

Grab a cab.
"Adonde?" he says. I
should have stayed on the damn plane,
my visa's good, travel agent trails
stranger through South American skies.
That's the glamour life—how to explain jet
set whimsy without seeming an ax murderer? I stay
with plans: Foz Do Iguazu, Las Cataratas,
solarium boat under the Falls.

Actually Alberto invited me to Bahia, his final destination.
Frankly, I thought he was kidding. Had I known he was serious,
would I have gone? No, my luggage was in Buenos Aires.
Besides, Alberto and I would see each other again. That was
part of the Herr Baer plan—that I should seek out an old Swiss
coot and end up with a South American child.

4) Argentina Te Quiero

Alone in Buenos Aires con Coca Cola,
cafe solo, a confiteria on the corner
Entre Rios and Belgrano. Why here? Argentina?
Solamente. A family town, padres y madres,
teenagers smoking. Me—no familia, no ninos,
mi ex-esposo, I read here in NY paper
is in a big play. Paula once said, "Imagine
if he gets rich and famous and
you've left him." Across the street a sign,
"Argentina Te Quiero," New York Te Quiero,
not the same, I walk
"Together Forever" blasting from
Avenida de Florida record stores. I think of
strangers, the one I married,
the one on the 7:05 Buenos Aires to Iguazu.

I could end up alone the rest of my life on foreign continents.
I haven't even seen Peter for 15 months. Maybe it's time to
take action into my own hands. I'll improve my German, fly to
Frankfurt, rent a car, drive to Eschenburg—have a talk with his
mother. Mothers can never resist women truly in love with
their sons.

5) Upper Ditmars Boulevard

In Queens, always the same, I hear
    the el cascade into Ditmars station.
No Alberto, no horseradish,
    safe on the couch, I type:
        Dear Alberto: I've had a crush
        on you since Iguazu.
        Let's meet, you'll like me.
        I'll fetch you wild beasts
        and never leave you
        at the mercy of trifles.
    My checks bounce all
over town. I see on the news:
Queens woman axed to pieces in vacant
    lot (not my neighborhood) and a plane
crash in Argentina.

6) Black Clouds

30 nights from Iguazu, Alberto calls,
    just back from Brasil when
New York is steaming, airless, Queens beaches
    closed from medical waste and sewage.
"Come down this weekend," but I have no tan,
    no clothes, no flash, but he's leaving
for Europe next week!

He's going backpacking! Staying at youth hostels! Oy vey—
just how young is he? 19—I'm 32, Peter's 46, 14 points one
way. 13 the other. Whenever I asked Peter to run off with me,
his standard answer was, "Yes, and in 5 years you'll dump me
for some young guy."

Airplanes! Jet fumes!
Landing lights! Don't fly off again,
damn it—stay in Bethesda, a shuttle flight
away, every half hour on the hour
and the half hour—more frequent than the
GG Brooklyn Queens Crosstown.
But he's all I've thought about—
destiny's long approach.
On Friday, I'm at the airport—
6:30 shuttle, departed, on time, 7:30
on time, an electrical storm approaches,
but they say we'll make it out.

7) Dover Beach

Alone con Alberto, black trees, night,
"I wanted to follow you," I say,
"Why didn't you?" he says. I say, "You can't
follow someone on a whim."
"Why not?" he says.

At 19, you can do anything you want. Why not 32? Why not
46? Who makes these rules, Germans, that's who!

Brasil, Argentina,
New York City, Maryland loam!
Finally we kiss among tree bark mosquitos. Let's stay!
Make the airplanes go away!
Hide in the house, lock doors,
chain ourselves to the radiators,

renounce the world! Nothing—
    only runway after runway,
dim lights from dimmer cities.

*Alberto's too young to know the radiator game, and I won't
teach it to him even though I went down with that idea,
thinking it was the only game we had to play. But modern
houses in Bethesda don't have radiators. He wouldn't want to
learn it anyway.*

8) No Ideas But In Things

Alone in Bethesda, alone with Alberto's
    blue quilt, Heineken can pencil
holder, German desk lamp, photos (Alberto
    sailing off Brasil coast, who's this?
Girlfriend?), bookcase without many
    books—school texts, economics, sports
trophies, medals, Walt Whitman High School
    yearbook,

*Alberto's in his brother's room (the family's in Colombia). We
didn't exactly have a fight—nothing got that far. It's OK, I can
be Zen about it, besides, I'm fascinated by his possessions.
This is his life, this is how he lives, and it has nothing to do
with me.*

            clothes in closet taunt me,
    "We're busy—who let you in here anyway?
        Go back to Queens." I couldn't
agree more.

*Alberto's life is not a life I should be interrupting, one way or
the other, good or bad. Peter's on the other hand, I should be
interrupting, good or bad. His life is my life, damn it.*

Peter's a coward and wants to do nothing but wait, like waiting in some hateful Beckett play. That's it, I'm going to march right into Frankfurt with heavy artillery and turn the place to rubble (Peter remembers when it was really rubble, he always said, "Frankfurt and I grew up together.")—hold him prisoner, then offer up the Marshall Plan.

       Desire splinters
    into lawns, Malls, cheerful cars,
DC discotheques, VCRs and unused
      Nonoxynol condoms.

So that's what broke Peter and me up—a dose of chlamydia. And where did it come from? Peter said he didn't have it, but that's impossible! If I had it, he had it—there was no one else! I asked my doctor about this, I said, "Leon, what gives?" He said, "Maybe you really didn't have it. Maybe the lab made a mistake. Maybe it was yeast." But I blamed Peter, and he blamed me.

9) Blame It On Rio

Who good looking stranger driving
    me across Potomac, what state now?
Maryland, Virginia? What country, jungle, city
Manhattan transit stop underground or el in
    Mass Transit of life? "Face it,"
Alberto says, "We made a mistake."

"Face it," Peter said, "we made a mistake—thinking we could do this with so many miles between us." I got hysterical, made a jerk of myself, bawling and beating against a Steigenberger Airport sign.

    I don't make mistakes! Not sitting
alone in Queens with horseradish, quitting

job, ballgame watch, Mookie at plate,
when cosmic wave jettisons across electric
el rail across rooftops—Lefkos Pirgos,
2-family houses, P.S. 85 into my window
with message—GO TO IGUAZU—THERE'S SOMETHING
THERE! No! No mistake! But maybe
a misdirection, a failure to
read the fine print. I say, "Blame it on Rio,"
as we pull to the curb.

Alberto drove me to National in his mother's car, some sort of
Japanese job. I felt like crying but wasn't sure why.
Disappointed, he said he'd wanted things to work out
splendidly (yea, yea, and I wanted to marry Herr Baer, move
to Brooklyn Heights). I kissed him good-bye on the cheek the
thought, "What trouble that would have been."

Morty Sklar
SMOKE

I have been aware
of river overhead
in the train to Queens,
and humans occupying seats
in the engineer cab.

The tunnel to Queens has
not yet collapsed
yet trains collided last year.

Smoke's pouring in the window,
changing faces

from looking down
to looking up,
from looking straight
to looking left and right.

What they're feeling
is what I
feel most of the time
without smoke
and I'm not afraid,
no more than usual.

1971

Mark Nickerson, photographer

Darryl Holmes
MONDAY

beyond these buildings
the sky is a hazy blue

a sparrow passes my window
without a sound

I have seen days like this
full of promise & ripe plums
full of God's sacred plans

white smoke rises from a factory
where men wait for a bell to go off

the trains are filled with weekend
stories
the sun is strong, and loving

I will enter a place
where poems are left at the door

where a man is a number
if he is lucky;

a name if he is not.

Mark Nickerson, photographer

A.J. Cipolla
THE BLACK KINGS IN LILY WHITE QUEENS

In the 1970s, Maurice Park was raped by construction on the Long Island Expressway: two baseball fields were lost as well as half the stone grandstand; the basketball courts were sliced by their length, rendering them useless except for maybe a game of horse; the tar field lost its third-base line and we had to learn to hit the ball toward center if we wanted to play there or else lose balls on the service road; and perhaps the biggest pain of all was caused by the new overpass that cut deep into the handball courts. There used to be ten courts; now there are two.

Ten years before that looting, Mayor John Lindsay referred to my town as "Lily white Maspeth." I was thirteen and still gullible enough to believe my mother's innocent interpretation.

"It's clean," she said looking down.

Trying to follow her view, I looked around at Long Island City, Woodside, Corona, Greenpoint, Middle Village and Ridgewood surrounding Maspeth and—to my eyes—they didn't seem to have any more dirt than we had.

In those early sixties, Maurice was ruled by the greaser-type teens and had its share of broken bottles, glass that would sparkle in the unkempt patches of grass, along with rotting leaves, doggy doo, and paper trash. The park office was frequently closed, and at night the older teens usually broke the locks on the little red brick building. The boys' toilets were victims of the worst vandalism—cherry bombs down the hatch, enough wet paper blobs hanging from the ceiling to make it look like stucco, and a smell that would hang around you all day if you ventured into the stalls. In spite of this, Maurice Park was a dream playground compared to what remains there today.

In those Eagle Scout Lindsay days, I was coming of age and making the park my second home. We used the courts for handball, but the absolute craze was a game called "strikeouts." It featured a square drawn on the wall with a large "S" in the middle—this was the box, the strike zone. Any pitch hitting the box was a strike. The ball was extremely lively; the *Spalding* and then the *Pensy Pinky* were the brand names. I preferred the *Pinky* because it seemed more durable; one good smack from a thin stickball bat could split a *Spalding* along its visible seam, and the balls were pretty expensive--27 cents, and later 53 cents, and still later 78 cents; but you can't buy them anymore.

The British invaded America. I grew my hair and combed it down with the other guys, wore the black boots and black turtlenecks, played drums in a band called the Satin Blues, which turned my ear into the beat that would in the years to follow become a marching band for the revolution. But in the early days it was all innocent: music, girlfriends and sports. Nobody my age was into drugs, although we had heard that the older crowd, Artie and Blaze and Skippy and their gang, once doo-woppers, now were turning on to pot. On the other side of this older crowd were Big Tommy, Kevin, Mike and their group, the Juiceheads (as we younger guys referred to them).

Both gangs of teens were violent and troublesome "hitters," but they were nice enough to us younger guys, and often would play some strikeouts with us before the sun set on Maurice. Then they would venture into darker forms of entertainment: most trotted their girls behind the grandstand for a quickie, more booze and more smoke; and then, even later in the night, they might get into some bathroom bashing, or burying somebody in the sandbox up to their neck, or maybe one of the girls would be tied to the flagpole so the boys could pick her pimples and blackheads . . . her screams could be heard by my bedroom's ears, as I lived only half a block from the park.

In the morning I would be the first one to arrive there—not counting the dog walkers whose pets were sniffing around madly at the discarded condoms from the night before; the grandstands especially were laden with them. I would go behind them to have my morning smoke; after breakfast a ciggy tastes good. Then I would wait for somebody—anybody—to show up. Hopefully somebody who was up for a game.

I remember the first time I met Henry. It was a warm, clear summer day. I was just finishing up my morning Lucky when he whizzed through the park on his bike. I had seen him a few times before, but I didn't know him by name. Henry stood out though, because he was black, the *only* black in Maspeth.

As most boys my age, I wore dungarees, tee shirt and Keds sneakers. But Henry dressed like an Ivy League student on the way to a tennis match, in a bright short-sleeve sports shirt, slacks and white boat sneakers—"sea dogs." Despite his dandy attire, Henry had the powerful body of an athlete. I watched as he pumped his muscular legs, calves bulging as he cycled up the hill exiting the park behind the grandstand.

I carried two *Pinkys* that day, one in the front pocket of my dungarees, the other I bounced as I made my way across the park to the handball courts, stickball bat slung over my shoulder. The courts were empty, available, and calling out, "Let the games begin." The sun was already strong; however, shade from a large tree was cast over the first court, offering protection from the ensuing heat. Pitching strikeouts could be an excruciating exercise and any assistance from the elements was appreciated.

First come first served. I took my position at the chalk pitching line on the first court and began waming up. As pitchers go, I was mediocre: I had a moderate fastball, and an underarm pitch that rose into the top portion of the box; my curve was nothing more than a miserable arc that sailed too obviously toward its destination. Players at my age hadn't really mastered the curveball, which when correctly thrown would break late and out of the strike zone or bust inside on the cuffs of the hitter. I tried one or two curves but soon bore down on my underarm riser, my best pitch. So intent was I on my deliveries, that I failed to notice Henry, who was leaning on the fence behind me, watching.

Upon retrieving a wayward pitch that was bouncing aimlessly on court two, I saw him there gripping the handlebars of his bike, which was balanced against the fence. Without speaking a word, he left the bike and walked around, toward me.

He was both taller and stronger than I, and at the time I believed that he was at least two years older. (I found out years later that Henry was actually one year younger; I was passing the summer that would deliver me into high school, while he was still in the lower grades.)

He picked up the bat and started to take some swings—I had second thoughts of how I would fare in a contest against him.

Suddenly he threw the bat straight up into the air.

(So, he's *that* familiar with the game, I thought.)

I caught it mid-stick as it came down over my head, and held it out for him to grab.

He placed his right hand over mine.

I placed my left over his.

We continued up the bat until nothing of it was left to grab but about a half inch of wood. Henry pinched this half inch with his fingertips, and as was the rule—which I was *very* surprised Henry knew—I was allowed one attempt to jar the bat from his grip by swinging it in one circular direction. I gave it a mighty twirl and it spun away from Henry like a pinwheel set free in the wind.

I had won the "choose" and earned "last-ups."

He retrieved the bat now with a happy anticipating expression and took his place against the wall. He was a righty.

Well now, what was I going to throw him? Obviously he had been watching me and knew my small array of pitches. He was certain to have seen my sidearm, as I was throwing that way for most of my warmups, and my fastball had lost its confidence so I couldn't challenge him with it, right off. That left the curveball, which I offered up for him to promptly smash. The ball egged and was only a pink blur as it ripped into the fence behind me.

"Single," I said. Henry nodded.

Although we never covered the ground rules—up to this point we hadn't even said a word between us—Henry seemed to know the boundaries. If his first hit had made it over the short fence it could have easily been a homer, which was way out beyond the benches of the tar field. One thing about a *Pinky*, when it gets hit it goes.

I considered myself lucky that he had only gotten the one-base hit, and I decided that the curveball was an obvious mistake. My second pitch was a sidearm riser. Henry swung through it, his bat slicing upwards, I noticed, an exact replica of his first swing. Well, I thought, he's a groove hitter, a perfect follow-through swing turning slightly up. This would be his demise. If he had any chance of hitting my riser, he would have to lift his elbows and get a higher cut. But he didn't adjust, and I struck him out easily.

My riser was a nasty pitch—but I must confess, it bordered on the point of being illegal. See, my release came from the right end of the pitching line with my arm nearly swiping the ground as I threw, toe scraping behind me, my momentum then carrying me two or three steps toward the batter. Now, it was questionable whether or not I kept my foot on the chalk line (the rubber) long enough. But, Henry never argued.

He was a terrific pitcher, although he only threw one pitch, a legitimate fastball that rose just before it reached the batter. He owned me with that pitch until the seventh inning when I miraculously tomahawked a ball that cleared the park office. We both ran for the ball because neither of us ever saw it bounce. We searched for nearly ten minutes before giving up. I had another ball and we could always come back and get this one later.

All through this, neither one of us spoke at all. In fact, my opponent and I seemed to take on a level of communication that I can't really explain.

Resuming the game silently, immediately—first pitch!—*bang!* I repeated my home run performance with another long shot that landed again near the park office. Henry was laughing as we ran to retrieve it. This time, though, we both had our eyes glued to the *Pinky*, which tried to roll away from us. Henry took up the task and ran the ball down; when he bent to pick it up and started jogging back he bounced two balls in front of him. Henry—what a find!

I was to meet him many times in the early morning that summer, and we played. We soon learned each other's pitching habits and the games took on larger and larger scores. This forced us to come up with different pitches and made us both better at the game. Our contests were battles of the mind as well as the body; at times I could swear I heard what he was thinking. Our games were charged with joy and a boyhood giddiness that comes from having pure *fun*; there was never any of the bickering or jealousy that boys often display during competition.

The game passed between us as easily as the soft summer's air through the holes in the fences that surrounded us.

1967 was the summer of love in cities like San Francisco and London, but no such peace consciousness settled on the psyche of the gangs that prevailed in Maurice. The older crowds —the Juiceheads and the Potheads-graduated-to-other-things— still reigned in the park, and us younger guys (although a few years older now) were to remain on the periphery of their frequent gang fights and hoodlum behavior. It seemed like at least once a week we were warned to stay out of the park because there was going to be another war. Sometimes the younger guys, some of my intellectually limited buddies, would take seats on the benches to watch the scraps.

Some idiots even placed bets on the individual match-ups. "I bet ya a chocolate soda Big Tommy takes Artie in five minutes."

I was never intrigued by this kind of danger and stayed away. My better instincts saved me one night as the losing gang (the Potheads) took their wrath out on my friends, and two were beaten up badly enough that they had to go to the hospital. I wasn't there so I can't tell you the gory details. But for weeks after that I heard the Potheads were still after me because I hadn't stuck up for them in their clash with the Juiceheads.

While the Juiceheads and Potheads warred regularly, something else was happening in Congress that would soon establish bonds of friendship between the two rival gangs. Desegregation was to affect our school, Grover Cleveland, with the tenderness and subtlety of a lightning bolt. Blacks—or negroes as they were then referred to by whites—from Bed Stuy were going to be bussed into our school, which bordered on Ridgewood Brooklyn and Maspeth Queens.

The Juiceheads and Potheads had drawn their forces together led by Artie and Big Tommy and had conspired with the white gangs of Ridgewood to meet hours before school started, taking with them their clubs, chains, brass knuckles, knives, zip guns and bravado dispositions.

The brutal events of that first day started at high noon. In the lunch room, Artie hurled a metal garbage can cover like a Frisbee at a table full of black kids. It hit an unassuming young girl in the head, and as she sat petrified in a pool of blood, all hell broke out around her.

Artie and the rest who started the brawl were ejected from school promptly, which only fitted their plan perfectly. Once outside school, the white gangs staged their ambush of the "niggers" that would take place after the final bell, when the blacks attempted to find their way back to their buses.

Waiting for those final few seconds to tick was similar to the ball descending on Times Square on New Year's Eve, only more sinister. I sat there thinking there was hope of us kids, black and white, sitting amicably side by side in a classroom. I didn't really understand any of it—after all, most kids, specifically the ones like Artie and Big Tommy, hated school passionately, and rarely—if ever—showed up. But here they were defending this same despised territory as if it were really a matter of life and death—or worse, honor. I wished I could explain to them the simple resolutions that formed naturally on my mind but were so hard to convey into words. Not that they would have listened to a shrimp like me anyway.

The faces of the teachers were drawn with fatigue and fear; they had held the world together with paper clips and chalk, and now that the last hour of the first day was upon us, they were prepared—and rightly so—to wash their hands of the crisis. It was three o'clock; class was dismissed.

My secret plan was to follow some adult—teacher or whomever, as long as they signaled authority—out of the school; hopefully I would get clear out of sight and make a run for my bus. But as I walked out of the school by the rear exit I saw no teachers, only Artie and Skippy and Blaze and the boys along with a large group of toughs from Ridgewood. Louie, another one of the Potheads, was also there. He recognized me and before I knew it he had placed a small but heavy lead pipe into my hands.

"Use this," he said, "the raisin-heads have thick skulls."

Then he put his arm around me and said that there were no hard feelings between us anymore even though I didn't stick up for him in his fight with the Juiceheads. A couple of them, Mike and Kevin (major alkies both) were here now under *Artie's* direction.

Can you imagine?

"Drugheads unite!"

We were joined together now under the white flag, regardless of our preferences for abusing substances. In Louie's eyes we were all now brothers, soldiers going to battle together.

When Louie turned away I swiftly hid the pipe inside my pants and under my shirt. A worse fate could not have befallen me, because now Louie was rushing me along with him to catch up with his gang. I realized that if I didn't stand up with him in his war with the "niggers" then I was going to find him my enemy.

"Behind the dugouts!" yelled Artie, and the crowd began running across the grass of the playground's baseball diamond. Louie dragged me along.

When the black students lined up for their buses along Himrod Street, they were attacked and hit with rocks by a crowd led by Big Tommy. A large group of black boys had remained at the main entrance of the school, and watched their brothers and sisters and friends being mugged. Now they retreated, running back through the school and out of a side entrance next to the gym. It led them right to the playground where Artie, Louie, Mike, Kevin and the rest of us guys from Maurice were waiting for them.

The numbers on both sides evened up pretty well, though there were more whites. It was hard to be certain because everything started so quickly. I blindly ran through the battle that broke out around me. Dust kicked up furiously and soon I found myself lost in this cloud of war. But I escaped all confrontation—nobody, black or white—seemed to pay attention to my existence. Dirt whipped into my face.

I rubbed my watery eyes at the sky. Through my distorted vision, I imagined a flock of helicopters from the Red Cross dropping crates hanging from parachutes—Care packages. The boys quit fighting and ran toward them. When the crates hit the field they broke open and brand new equipment spilled out: baseballs, bats, bases, and even uniforms, in sizes to fit all ... there were white shirts with blue letters in script that read: *Black Kings*; other crates contained shirts of red and white with *Maurice* written boldly across the chest. The boys began to don their uniforms and equipment. I felt in my pocket for the lead pipe and found a ball-strike clicker.

I was to be the umpire.

Although I presided over the event with honest intentions, I secretly was rooting for the Maurice team, and as a consequence I sympathized with the Black Kings when it came to a close call. But the white boys would understand, I hoped. Anyway, they were my *friends*.

It would be a great contest, a close game down to the last out, the last pitch. There would be magnificent plays in the field and long home runs hit. There would be hand slapping and cheers as boys dove for bases and kicked up the dust. And out of these grains of sand would be born a small amount of mutual respect; minute, but enough for a start.

In reality, before me was the future: pounding sounds, groans of nausea and screams of pain. I don't recall how long . . .

It went on until two police cars drove in through the playground gate. As the dust settled, I stood in the middle of the madness without a scratch, while a boy—who looked like Henry—lay dead.

When nobody was looking, I threw away the lead pipe.

Audrey Gottlieb, photographer

Audrey Gottlieb, photographer

Rudy Kikel
NECESSARY RELOCATIONS

I knew they couldn't tell on you if told
    in confidence that you had killed
someone or robbed a bank, but could I trust
    a priest from Sacred Heart with *this*?
I bore my weighty secret to the priest
    at a neighboring parish church
instead: "Bless me, father, for I have sinned."
    Would he have heard the like before?
"It has been about a month since my last
    confession." But my last good one—
how long ago was that? "These are my sins:
    I have been thinking about . . . boys . . .
wanting sex with them, I mean." Silence. Then:
    "What I'm going to ask you may seem
a little strange," he whispered in the dark—
    solicitously, much later
I realized—"but are you . . ."
                        Another
    pause. What inquiry was coming?
Was I addicted to my vice? Aware
    I was diseased? What requisite
for forgiveness would he insist upon—
    that I see a "shrink," swear never
again to place my soul in jeopardy
    or myself in a room alone
with a boy, have my parents contact him?
    I had steeled myself for any
question—any question other, that is,
    than the one he decided on
asking, than which I could imagine none,
    at the time, more mortifying,
nor, later, one more inevitable
    of a fourteen-year-old being
interviewed by the Lord's luminary

forced to operate, as he was,
from within a dim cubicle into
    which from behind an obscuring
screen and from out a dimmer cubicle
    still came words. "Are you," he went on,
"a girl or a boy?"

                    The Lord only knew!
    I wasn't sure I did. At least,
I knew how little I felt like the boy
    I was supposed to be! Perhaps
the devil knew, and the devil—that night,
    anyway—was a man waiting
in a car parked on the dark Forest Park
    and graveyard side of Myrtle
Avenue—connecting St. Pancras',
    which I had just left, and the end
of Glendale in which I lived—and who peered
    from a window, interrupting
my passage, to inquire whether I knew
    where Downing Street was. "No." I thought,
though: "Isn't there one in England—somewhere,
    anyway, other than Glendale."
The stranger followed up his first question
    with a second: how would I like
to go with him for a ride? I was not
    so naive not to know what *that*
meant! Who but the incarnate devil
    could this be then, placing himself
in my path and proposing to me fresh
    from the confessional what but
an acting out of crimes—and on Christmas
    Eve!—I had just been absolved from!
Though even at the time I remember
    thinking: why hasn't this happened
to me at *any other time*?

I got
my state of grace home, as it were,
intact, and myself back to concealing
the confusion in which I lived
from parents and all those friends in Glendale
who would have been appalled, *I just
knew*, had they been privy to my thoughts on
the mornings I would tuck a sheet
under my armpits, smooth it with both arms
down at my sides and imagine
myself dressed—in a strapless evening gown!
Or witnessed the apparition
I had created, after having rushed
upstairs—my parents having gone
out that night—swathed myself in their chenille
bedspread, bound it with my mother's
silver clasps at the "collar," and become—
or watched the mirror in her room
reflect—who was it? Cleopatra? *Some*
queen. Who was I? And what were we,
for that matter, Richie and I, when his
folks had stepped out and we commenced
the private showings we called "playing sheets"?
Girls! Weren't they the ones who got
to wear the pretty things, and what else did
I then want for myself except
to fit in with the boys—those dreamboats! *That*
was the problem: how to convince
the boys that I was one of them, who spent
so much of his time with the girls—
listening to the radio and learning
the new lindy steps *we*, the girls
and I—during those precious times I would
be asked to perform the service—
would later teach to *them*. I attended
to Glendale's feminine blossoms

on Dorothy Mistretta's stoop while boys
    played basketball before our eyes
across the street at P.S. 94.
    Boys: they were supposed to "go" with
girls, weren't they? How better to signal
    my desire that I be taken
for one of them—since I wasn't playing
    ball with them in the schoolyard—than
by doing what I already felt most
    comfortable doing: being
with girls—Nancy, Rory, Kathy, Carol,
    Gail Ann, Laurel, Joan, and the rest,
whom I took to our Confraternity
    dances, C.Y.O. roller rink
events, and weekend parties. And the girls
    were wonderful—such good dancers,
sympathetic—their one request seeming
    to be that for the length of time
we "went" together we be said to be
    "going steady." Pins, rings, ankle
bracelets made the rounds.

                                    How was I doing?
    How dismally I was failing
to make the desired impression became
    clear when Bob, the present boyfriend
of one of my "exes," Joan, and of young
    men coming to flower in our
crowd the most beautiful, on a Sunday
    morning advised me that he and
a lot of the other boys—arrayed just
    then behind him—all, I had thought,
my friends!—didn't like my "way of treating
    girls," and that although he would not
touch me then and there—after Mass, outside
    of church—I had "better watch out."

Thus began for me the memorable
   weeks during which he and Billy,
a frustrated, prospective attendant
   on my then current "flame," Kathy,
together would wait for me at a bus
   stop and threaten to "fix my ass"—
softening me for a kill, or hoping
   the appropriate scare tactics
might terrorize me into behaving
   in ways to them desirable.
Of the gang I wished to join, in any
   case, I had become an outcast.

Where had I gone wrong? Finally I came
   to see myself as the boys must
have seen me: in the time not spent with them
   in athletic competition
pressing my advantages on the girls
   in whose eyes they had hoped to shine:
lindy skills and amiability
   engendered, ironically,
by my lack of acquisitive desires.
   I passed from one to another
girl—why not? I saw no reason to keep
   one for myself, who liked them all!—
tying up affections and leaving boys
   often in possession of what
must have seemed my "discards." So my modus
   vivendi called into question
the necessity of "having" a girl
   of one's own at the very time
I seemed also to be having them all!
   Wanting to be "one of the boys,"
I had become cock of the walk, the buck
   other bucks would have to lock horns
with in order to secure for themselves

a piece of the territory—
but also a "flirt," a breaker of hearts,
   Glendale's ruthless "lady-killer"!

Mountain king, then, despite—and because of—
   myself, the king gave up his ground
on the night Bob, Glendale's new champion
   of trifled-with little women,
ran across me on Doran Avenue
   and delivered the punch I had
been promised, the rough touch that finally came.
   As I lay breathlessly before
him, his position seemed to be asking
   again the old question, now put
to me another way: "A boy or girl,
   what are you?" That is, would I fight?
And boys, or these boys in Glendale, it dawned
   on me suddenly, were willing,
eager, perhaps even forced to fight for
   and because of girls—and I was
not. Looking at the brawny piece of meat
   hovering over me, prone though
it had just proved itself to violent attack—
   or was it me sprawled at Bob's feet
and all my calculations which were just
   now painfully undergoing
one?—I despaired of ever getting Bob
   or any of the boys I knew
to fight—not with, but for and over me—
   as he was gallantly prepared
to do for Joan. Doomed—
                              or suddenly free
   to operate unrestricted
by gloomy alternatives Sacred Heart
   and Glendale had arranged for me,
to enter onto—what should I call it

else who had as yet no names for
the possibilities that I hoped would
    present themselves in place of those
I was leaving behind—but the Downing
    Street of my Imagination?
A few days later, dolled up in a black
    boat-neck shirt I had selected
for the occasion—tight across the chest,
    tapered down the sides—I hitchhiked—
my first time ever!—to Rockaway Beach,
    along Woodhaven Boulevard.
I knew what I wanted to have happen.
    Eventually a car slowed
down, stopped. A man peered out. I was sixteen
    and about to be blown away.

Rhina Espaillat
REPLAY

A dusty courtyard of the inner city:
Sunday, September, nineteen thirty-nine.
Three seven-year-old girls, huffing and panting,
are taking turns jumping an old clothesline.

A younger neighbor stands by to be invited.
He wears a skullcap, white shirt, black pants, old shoes.
Cathy—our leader, because the rope is hers—
is placid: "We're not supposed to play with Jews."

I am foreign-born; I don't quite know what Jews are,
and think, in my ignorance, that everybody's friends,
but sense, from the sudden aging of his eyes,
something's been said for which there are no amends.

Dorothy scans the ground—we're in her yard—
and I wonder if there's something I should say;
but what? and to whom? And so I fidget
with the knotted ends of the rope, and he goes away.

And that's all of the story, as it happened.
But in my dream we always call him back
to say the words that heal our common exile
and switch the looming future from its track.

Rhina Espaillat
PURIM PARADE

Who's this coming now?
Queen Esther in tinsel wig;
two sheiks on skate boards;

Tyrannosaurus
Rex clutching his mother's hand;
Death striding on stilts;

A coven of small
witches shreiking in Spanish;
the Temple Youth Group

twirling gilt batons,
shivering in their red tights;
Saint Benedict's School;

the Emerald Band
elegant in kilts, bagpipes
skirling Hatikvah.

Barbara Unger
ON 69th STREET, WOODSIDE

Seventy years ago
in this slum parish
neighbor set
against neighbor,

legacy of Blacks
and Tans, local legends,
partisan feuds.

From the open windows
the lilting prattle,
broken Yiddish
strained affinities.

The street still stands
all the immigrant houses
unmoved from my childhood

the trough of the past
runs through these streets

children trotting home for dinner
the postman counting letters
A Korean Presbyterian Church
on the corner, bodega,
falafel, dolmades,

but it's the smell of fresh-cut
grass, the old garden smells
that make me restless
for my old epitaphs.

Shall I knock?

Who will let me in?

Barbara Unger
TWO GOLD STARS

During the years before World War II, I was forbidden to pass in front of the Murphys' house. All I could do was observe their frame row house from a distance and imagine the mysteries that lay behind its locked door and lace-curtained windows. If I were a boy, things might be different. Boys could fly into the wild blue yonder and climb high into the sun. But girls had to sit safely on the stoop and play potsie or jacks. Nor was I permitted to read the comic strip "Little Orphan Annie" because my father would not permit an anti-New Deal paper in the house. Because of the Annie-Semites, I couldn't read about Daddy Warbucks and Sandy. Mother said there were Annie-Semites everywhere but especially on Ellis Place. Because of the Annie-Semites, my permissable borders in the Irish stronghold of Woodside, Queens, remained—to the east— the Brennans' stoop, and to the west my grandfather's shabby rose garden.

After a large Sunday meal of brisket and kugel, the men retired to the parlor to argue politics and life at the factory. During those long Sunday visits, my mother entertained me with fairytales told in an Irish brogue so authentic that one could scarcely discern it from Mrs. Brennan's. The Brennans next door had become our family's staunchest defenders on the block in the 1920s when my grandfather first planted his flag on Ellis Place. From the open windows of the Brennans came the lilting accents of Galway and Cork. The Irish brogue was, in fact, the first speech I could recall. As the eldest daughter of the first assimilated Jewish family in the neighborhood, back in 1925, my mother spoke in Yiddish only when she didn't want me to understand what she meant.

Imagine my horror when my mother announced one Sunday that I was too old for fairytales. Such a thing seemed impossible. Beneath the spell of my mother's tales, I fell into a reverie inhabited by tinkers and elves, giants and crones. The very air on Ellis Place seemed filled with bog monsters, shamrocks and harps that came to visit in that nether world between sleep and waking.

"Please, Ma, just one," I pleaded.

"Have a heart, Hannah. No stories. You'll grow up simple." But I begged so, that finally my mother put down her knitting and agreed to tell me one more. The final one. The very last. It was the story of her girlhood friend Mary Elizabeth, the original author of these tales. Vindicated, I curled up in my mother's lap and fell under the spell of her voice.

The story was this:

They were born a week apart; she and Mary Elizabeth. They wrote songs and stories and made music together on the parlor piano. Mary Elizabeth taught her jigs and reels and this verse of a song:

Apple jelly, lemon and a pear
Gold and silver she shall wear
Gold and silver by her side
Take Mary Elizabeth for a bride

"Oh what a sweet voice she had! Clear as a bell. We were like sisters. That close."

"Then what happened?" I yawned sleepily.

"I can't say."

"Where is she now?"

"She moved away. Anyway," said my mother, "I've told you too much already." She removed the knitting needles from my bear-like grip and put them on the table. "You're too old for these tales, and it's time for bed."

Fascinated by the idea of my mother's friendship with the author of the fairytales, I searched for her photo in the family album. And I found them both—two wraiths in flapper dresses and bobbed hair shingled to a dark shaved point that tapered down the back of the neck. Before that, there were two school-girls in high-button shoes and middy blouses—my mother and Mary Elizabeth. Until that moment, my mother's girlhood in Woodside was like a closed door through which nobody could squeeze.

Only Mrs. Brennan could shed more light on the story. Over milk and cookies, Mrs. Brennan was flattered to be given a chance to recount the local legends. She lowered her well-corseted figure into a chair and began:

"First off, the block was full of feuds. The one between your grandfather and Murphy wasn't half of it, let me tell you."

"Tell me about Mary Elizabeth."

A sad smile flickered on her broad rosy face. "Fun and flashy in her own way, as you'd expect of a redhead. Always the life of the party—reciting, singing and dancing. We all thought she was headed for the stage."

"And my mother?"

"The quiet one. She could bide her time. She was a pianist and scholar. At least that's what we thought back then. When she left school to go to work on Wall Street, she bobbed her hair. Your grandfather wasn't the kind to ask his children to cling to old-country ways here in the new land. After work, the two girls began to go out dancing the Charleston at the ballrooms downtown but Mary Elizabeth had to sneak around her father when he forbade her to go out." Mrs. Brennan pressed her lips together and her fiery old eyes glowed with remembrance. "Oh, inseparable they were. Until the old man put a stop to all that."

"Grandpa?" I questioned.

"Oh, no. It was Old Man Murphy, Mary Elizabeth's father, who put an end to it. Threw the poor girl out of the house, he did, the old stinker."

The war in Europe and the Pacific dragged on. It was a long war, chewing at the edges of everybody's life. All of my uncles except Uncle Phil, who was 4F because of a bad ear, went off to fight the Nazis. During these years I kept vigil on the deserted house where Old Man Murphy lived. The house seemed sinister and alien to me.

One day when my mother was out of earshot, my Uncle Phil lowered his voice and swore to me in secrecy. His face was solemn and inscrutable.

"Do you want to know the true story of Old Man Murphy?"

To protect Mrs. Brennan, I pretended utter innocence.

"Did you know that goose-stepping Nazis with guns and helmets once marched down these very streets?" he whispered.

The idea of real Nazis marching down Woodside's streets was, to me, far more fascinating than any distant war news.

"More likely you'd call them Nazi sympathizers. For years they had a club of sorts down the street. This neighborhood was a stronghold of the German-American Bund. Some even sided with the Kaiser during the first war. After Murphy got pensioned off for drinking on the job, he put in his lot with them. After a few beers, he was right up there bragging with the rest. One night, after a drinking bout, they and Old Man Murphy burned a cross in our yard. Don't tell your mother I told you. It's not supposed to be told. But your grandfather outwitted the old bastard. Put a big American flag in the attic window. It's still there, to remind Murphy that he's not forgotten or forgiven."

"Is Old Man Murphy still alive?" I asked.

"The wife died some years ago and William and Kevin, the sons, broke with the old man's politics as soon as they were old enough to think for themselves. They were the first on the block to enlist. Just walk up the block and look in the window and you'll find the upshot of it all."

Just then, I heard my mother enter and stop at the door. She had overheard the end of the conversation. Her face was citron and her eyes flashing like semaphores.

"So he's already making you crazy with his talk about this street," she said, glancing up at the ceiling for an answer. I was banished to the kitchen. A few moments later I heard my uncle slam the back door. Then it opened again and I could hear voices. *Not for the child ... all over ... years ago ...* and Yiddish, the language my mother saved for adult secrets. Little puddles of Yiddish again and finally my mother's voice. *Annie-Semites.* Then silence and the door slamming again.

Mrs. Brennan turned out to be a veritable treasure-trove of information on neighborhood life in the years before I was born.

The story went like this:

"Mary Elizabeth moved into a women's hotel in Manhattan. She was starting to lead a fast life, singing in a few lounge rooms where the men would pay her a great many attentions. It was a life she didn't want but the Old Man refused to let her return home. He called her a slut, a slattern; all those old-country words a father can use to shame a young girl. That's when Mary Elizabeth sought refuge with your mother next door in your grandfather's house. That did it. When one of your uncles took her out to the movies (some said he was sweet on her) the Old Man came out with a club and stood in front of your grandfather's house, yelling how he'd see her in hell first rather than living with Christ-killers. All of us on the street would have taken the girl in until Murphy threatened to burn us all out if we didn't give her back. After that she wouldn't set a foot on this street. Not as long as the Old Man was alive."

"And she never returned?" I inquired with bated breath.

"Not to my knowledge, darling. She's not once shown her face here in all those years. Some said she went to ruin and drink, poor thing, but none could say for sure. Now you take a Lorna Doone cookie and run along like a good girl and, if your mother asks you where you got this tale, don't tell her it was from me, mind you."

Inside the parlor, dinner was about to be served. Around the table sat my grandfather, his second wife Chava, her daughter Lilly, my Uncle Phil and my parents. At the head of the table, shawl on his shoulders and prayer book in hand, my grandfather presided.

"Where have you been, young lady?" my mother whispered.

"Nowhere," I whispered back.

My father took a sip of seltzer and belched.

"Cover your mouth and say excuse me," hissed my mother.

"I hope you haven't been up to the end of the block."

"For Chrissakes, Fanny," said my father, "why can't the kid walk up the block?"

"Don't tell me you've forgiven the vicious old Annie-Semite?"

"All that happened years ago. The old lady passed on. The war is almost over. Have a heart," said my uncle.

"Ask Mrs. Brennan. She'll tell you about Murphy's kind," said my mother, her nostrils flaring.

"Can't we just bury the dead?" asked my uncle. "We're all supposed to believe all men are brothers."

"With all due respect to brotherhood, some people don't act in accord with your rosy slogans," said my mother. This was followed by a squabble in Yiddish and the word *luftmenschen*, an epithet meaning "idealist" or "dreamer." My mother threw down her napkin and left the table. I heard her at the parlor piano, vigorously attacking Gershwin's "Rhapsody in Blue." Finally, we began to eat.

Armed with my new knowledge, I decided to sit on Mrs. Brennan's stoop after dinner. I recalled my uncle's words about walking up the block and finding an answer in the window. I rose, drawn towards the Murphy house as if it were a magnet. But one doesn't walk past long-sealed doors without trepidation. My heart beat in terror and I looked over my shoulder to make sure nobody could see me. When I arrived, I realized that the forbidden house was just like ours, a narrow frame house with a Dutch gable. Weed and cattail grew in the yard.

In the window I saw them. Two Gold Stars, the kind that signified dead war heroes. They were like military flashcards on the inside of my eyelids, as I remembered what my uncle told me about William and Kevin. Just then, a broken shade flew up and a figure appeared at the door. He was a burly man with iron-grey hair and inflamed pale eyes. He appeared to be drunk and very unsteady on his feet. We faced each other for an instant. Riveted to the spot by fear, all of the stories I had heard about this old man mixed in a mad flurry in my head.

"Trying to sneak up on me, eh?" he said.

"I came to see the Gold Stars in the window."

"Well, get the hell out of here and mind your own business," he said. For a second I thought he might come after me.

"You're Fanny's girl, aint'cha?"

I nodded.

"There's nothing for you here. What are you standing there for? Do you have some business with me?"

"No," I said.

"Then get out of the way." He came towards me and I turned and ran. My feet carried me back down the block towards my grandfather's house. The sky was dark; crooked halos of the street lights were coming on; it was probably past my bedtime. I was in for it this time, and I knew it. Any prospects for reprieve were dim. Before going in, I sat on the Brennans' stoop, contemplating my punishment.

Two black-laced oxfords settled beside me. I looked up and saw my Uncle Phil. Playfully he ruffled my hair and gave me a handkerchief to wipe my dirty face. He took my hand. I loved the calloused feel of my uncle's palm, and felt secure in the knowledge of his protection.

"You saw them?"

I nodded weakly.

"The boys were blown to bits flying somewhere over Germany and the Pacific. Isn't it time to let bygones be bygones?" he said, looking up to the ancient and colorless American flag that hung in our attic window.

"Old Man Murphy shook his fist at me."

"Murphy is just a poor old drunk filled with guilt and sorrow. Pay no mind to him. A closed chapter." Then his face took on a faraway look.

"It's about Mary Elizabeth, isn't it?"

"With the sons, it was politics," mused my uncle. "But with the daughters it was different." He sighed and his eyes grew dim as he stared into the distance. "Come on, Hannah, it's getting late. I think it's time we headed back."

"But what was she like?"

"In those days, girls were expected to be . . . well, we called them 'home girls'. Mary Elizabeth wasn't that kind."

On the steps my uncle held out his handkerchief once more so that I could scrub my face and blow my nose.

My mother was still at the piano producing cascades of sound. She finished with a flourish of arpeggios and looked up at me and my uncle, left the piano and took up her knitting. I could tell that she knew I had challenged her wall of secrecy and that I wouldn't be forgiven for it. Her eyes were dangerously hot.

"Now don't tell me you're going to ask for another make-believe story," she said. "You're too old for fairytales. They'll only make you simple. Let me warn you. Soon we'll be moving and you'll start a new school. Do you think anyone will want to play with a grown child who still likes fairy tales?"

"Where are we moving?"

"Four beautiful rooms in the northwest Bronx near the park. Your father, thank God, is doing better now—the factory is starting to bring in a good income. I think he's finally ready to sign a lease." *Jab jab jab jab* her knitting needles flew.

'When?"

"Sooner than you think," she said firmly. I glanced as if for the first time at my mother, magician, weaver of spells, impersonator, but her mouth was set firmly. No stories. Rapidly, she cast stitches on her curved needles.

"Please, just one?"

"None." *Jab jab.* Her face was red with determination. "Let's go into the parlor and hear what your father has to say about the war." Not even a war and two Gold Stars could form a truce for her silent and unforgiving heart.

As the tides of the war began to turn, my uncles, handsome rakes in khaki, returned unharmed and I informed my mother that fairy tales were baby stuff. I wanted no more of them. In

The Bronx I felt free of the Annie-Semites of Ellis Place. They receded into the night-blue ceiling of the Loew's Paradise where I surrendered to celluloid fantasies. In my dreams I was a pilot. Beneath my wing guns, Messerschmidts smoked and wheeled in flame. I gave the thumbs-up and roared off to death and glory.

On those weekend trips to my grandfather's house in Woodside, I still sat on the Brennans' stoop or else in our tiny rose garden. That summer the light in Woodside was a brilliant ocher-yellow but the dark spell of the street remained. In our attic, the faded banner still flew. Years later, shortly before his death in the nineteen-fifties, my grandfather finally removed it. When I walked up to the deserted Murphy house, I thought I still heard Old Man Murphy climb creaking stairs to empty rooms, rummage through bureaus, trace mattress gullies for the shapes of his dead children, spill yet another drink over his shirt. Sometimes I thought I saw them behind the torn shrouds of curtains—the two flying aces and Gold Star heroes in olive drab, their planes spinning out of control, and the scarlet daughter lost forever.

Maureen McCafferty
ADMISSIONS

Hallie has driven her grandfather to the Queens General Hospital to get the battery changed on his pacemaker. They are sitting in the very crowded admissions room with time to pass, so her grandfather begins at his usual place: "I'm not really your grandfather you know. Your grandmother was married before she married me. She married me because I had a house and she had her two girls and nowhere to live. I'm not sure we're married at all. I don't remember any ceremony. And I can't find anyone who was there. But we've been together fifty years. Some people don't live fifty years."

Hallie does know all of this and says so. She and her sisters Nora and Tessa have grown up with his stories. Her grandfather goes on to other things. "I haven't slept with your grandmother in fourteen years."

This is a new angle. "Why's that?" Hallie asks.

"Because she has too many mechanical parts. Might break her. And she's hard to patch now, at her age. We're very old."

Hallie's grandmother has two artificial hips. She got them a while ago when her own hips gave out. Unlike most people who recover remarkably from the procedure, Hallie's grandmother had nearly no hip bone left by the time the operations were done so she's never really recovered, though she is a remarkable recoverer. (Unlike some of the rest of the family, Hallie's grandmother has recovered from worse than surgery and artificial parts in her life, just ask her daughters and granddaughters.)

Hallie is vaguely thinking some of this as her grandfather tells her, "That doctor of your grandmother's did a great job getting those parts in her at all. You remember how she just collapsed at work—worked till her bones gave out. Funny thing how she worked for the bone doctor and then it was her bones that went on her. Makes you think about the choices you make, or at least about the jobs you have—I had at least a hundred in my day. One was in a crematorium. Gave me a great

131

respect for fire. Catholics aren't supposed to be cremated, you know. They think you won't have your body for Judgment Day. Think that means you won't be judged? Never heard any of them say that." Their family is Catholic, though all dissenters in one way or another, except for their grandmother.

Hallie begins to notice how people are looking at her, as though she is supposed to stop her grandfather from talking so much, as though she should tell him that he's too loud, as though she, at least, should be embarrassed. Hallie's not. She has great respect for her grandfather's talking. It's shattered many of the deadly silences she's grown up with. His talking has filled more than a few of these silences with some strange stories and some even odder ideas but that's always been better than the nothing, or the secrets.

Hallie's never been able to find a reason for all the secrets, except that her grandmother is from the same small square of County Monaghan Ireland as their grandfather and though her grandmother's lived most of her life among the millions of people in New York, she's never been able to shake off the small town worry of what the neighbors will know and think. Hallie and her sisters, who have lived their whole lives in Queens, moving through many of its neighborhoods, living among all nationalities of people, know that the neighbors mostly worry about themselves and want you to worry mostly about yourself too.

The hospital admissions room is very hot and crowded. It's January, so Hallie and her grandfather have heavy coats with them, on their laps. Her grandfather is filling his pipe, getting tobacco flakes all over himself and the floor, not paying attention to the mess as he goes on with thoughts about the Church (one of his great subjects) and death. "What does the Church think you have left of yourself after you rot? Of course, they don't talk about rotting. They talk about everlasting life, but that sounds like wishful thinking to me."

"You believe in spirits," Hallie says, knowing this from all the stories her grandfather has told her about the spirits, and shadow gods, the *daoine sidhe*, in Ireland. Her grandfather has told her stories about seeing the shadows, the fairies, when he was a boy. He doesn't tell these as make-believe stories. He believes in the Celtic gods, as his father and mother before him believed.

"Yes, I do believe in spirits—doesn't mean I'll be one. I think we get what we deserve. That's why we rot."

He's in a foul mood, Hallie thinks, ready to let it go. But her grandfather's not easy to stop once he gets going on religion. "Religions don't make too much sense if you really look at them," he tells Hallie. "Guess that's why most don't ask you to. *Just believe us*, they tell you. *Have faith*. You think that's enough?"

This is a serious question. But Hallie's too hot in this over-crowded, over-heated room and too tired now to think about faith. "I don't know. Enough for what?"

"Enough to be saved? Is faith enough to be saved? What did you think we were talking about?"

"I was still picturing rotting in the ground."

"Well, missionaries didn't go all over the world talking about rotting in the ground. Who'd want to listen to that? They knew how to sell: they talked about being saved, having *faith!* That's what they told people, didn't they?"

"Probably."

"That's right. And they told people that what they already believed in was foolish. Well, it's all foolish and all the same. Be very careful what kind of things you believe and what kind of jobs you take—could affect your whole life. Your Uncle Daniel was a missionary on some desert island that didn't even have a post office. You couldn't even send him a letter if you wanted. Well, he's dead now—" Hallie knows her grandfather is about to spit tobacco juice, till he catches himself, remembering he's in a hospital. "I guess that island has a post office now," he says, his skinny legs crossed, one foot swinging. "It surely has a Catholic church. I'd rather get mail. Yes, all over the world, not even expanding services, you know—making the mail or the buses better, just making people give up what they know to believe something else, something they don't know at all except for what you're telling them. The Church made people give up being healers you know, in Ireland. My own father's greatgrandmother had to hide from the priests. And then the priests had to hide from the bastard British soldiers. All ridiculous. Terrible things. I'm going pretty far back you know. I'm very old."

"I know," Hallie answers, trying to listen to the names being called on the loudspeaker.

"Did I ever tell you the story of my father bringing the child from his coma? My father was a healer, you know. Did I ever tell you that story?"

"Yes," Hallie answers, "but it's a good one."

"It is. I was only thinking of cures because of your grandmother's bones, because of them falling apart on her. Terrible thing. There's not a thing the matter with me that a few wires and batteries won't help. The last time they changed my batteries I had two Chinese doctors who let me watch everything they did. They had a mirror on the wall above their heads and I could look up there and see them make a little slit in me to get at the mechanical pieces. Amazing thing, not like watching yourself at all. They worked fast, those doctors." Her grandfather puts his pipe in his mouth but takes it out quickly, to say, "If they could make bone and not have to use the plastic and ball bearings for the fake parts it would be better for your grandmother. Someday I guess. When I was born you died when you broke your hip—that's how old people died, horses too. We plowed with the horse and rode the mule to town when I was born. I'm very old, you know."

Then he's quiet a while, thinking about something, swinging his skinny leg. Hallie isn't ready when he tells her (and everybody in the room), "I've done terrible things in my life, Hal, terrible things. It's awful to face that when you're going to die."

"You're here for new batteries. You're not going to die."
Hallie knows she is dismissing what her grandfather wants to
tell her, which is what he's always told her: the truth, but she
is in a crowded room with many strangers and she does not
want to hear his confession now.

"I'm not going to last much longer. How old do you think
people get?" he laughs. He pulls a long smoke on his pipe and
then tells her, "I'm more than ninety years old. There's things
I've done you wouldn't believe. Whatever God there is, isn't
going to forgive me."

Hallie has her doubts that there's any God at all but she
doesn't think that is the right path to comfort right now. Ad-
justing her coat, which seems to be getting heavier in her lap,
she crosses her legs and swings one a bit, and offers, "God,
whoever she or he is, surely doesn't want anyone to suffer. God
wants to love us, no matter what we've done. If we're sorry,
we're forgiven. Are you sorry?"

"I have a feeling it's not that easy."

Hallie wants to say something to make her grandfather laugh
but he's too serious. This isn't like him, and now she is beginning to resent that he has started this here, of all places, with
her. She doesn't want to know what horrible, unforgivable
things her grandfather's done. He's never done any of them to
her, or her sisters. They love him. Without question, without
condition. No forgiveness needed. Through all the crazy, confusing, secret times in their family, and there have been more
than a few, their grandfather has been the healer. He's loved
them without condition; he's watched over them, he's helped
them, without being asked. Whatever they've needed, he's giv-
en. And he's given them a part of themselves they couldn't
have known from anyone else, for their grandfather has told
them stories about himself and his life. He knew firsthand and
taught them as though they knew firsthand too, the world he
was born into, the first days of this century in Ireland: the
world of stone houses, thatched roofs, shadow gods, charms,
cures, witches, healers, songs, land eviction, revolution, colon-

ization, the brutal rule of the British (over a land with nothing but an identity to lose and die for). He's given Hallie and her sisters part of the people they've come from. That's what Hallie feels right now. And she's angry that he doesn't know this, that he doesn't see how much his life with them has mattered. She wants to tell him that.

A nurse is calling names and people are shifting in their chairs as they are being told what rooms to go to.

Hallie is about to say some of this to her grandfather, when they hear his name being called, not hearing the room he's supposed to find. They gather their things.

"Let's go," he says, moving down the hall.

Hallie notices how frail her grandfather is. He is more than ninety years old and weighs about ninety pounds. He is in his best suit, vest, gray felt hat. She can't follow him into the room where the doctor is taking him. Be careful, she wants to tell him, wondering where the mirrors are. "Be careful," she says, as if he can do anything but let what will happen happen.

He smiles as he always does to steady Hallie whenever she is afraid.

Clark Blaise
BEYOND THE BRIDGE AND TUNNEL:
THE QUEENS INDIANS

We heard a lot about sober immigrant virtues in the 1988 election: about Ellis Island, southern Europe, neighborhoods, saving, discipline and reverence for education. We heard about the American Dream, and how to fulfill it. And above all, we heard about family. Maybe we even heard a little too much about large, intact, extended families and about piety and morality. Maybe all those testimonials to Old World diligence left us envious, bitter, or suspicious. Immigrants, let's face it, are unhip, uncool, the epitome (if they live in New York's outer boroughs, or New Jersey) of "Bridge and Tunnel" behavior. Mainstream America, according to the election at least, sees itself as just a little looser, a little less driven.

I propose, then, an updating of all those "Moonstruck" images, those John Travolta movies, those Brighton Beach memoirs, Ellis Island-Little Italy-Brooklyn-Bronx-Lower East Side souvenirs in our collective trunks. Let us suggest a brief weekend stroll down the sunny side of immigration. Same old virtues, same naked pursuit of money and advancement, but in a very different package. The Dream seems right, all over again.

Pick a bright, warm Saturday or Sunday and go to 74th Street and Broadway, Jackson Heights, Queens. It's easy to get to—half an hour, 13 stops on the elevated Number 7 train out of Times Square (for Mets fans, that's six stops before Shea Stadium)—easy to inspect, a pleasure to sample. Those thirty minutes are thirty years removed from the megabuck commercial feeding frenzy of Manhattan. Jackson Heights is next door to Mario Cuomo's Corona, far south and much downscale from Michael Dukakis' Brookline.

If New York is still a potent attraction for immigrants, a doorway to America (it now ranks second to a booming Pacific rim, Latin-overland Los Angeles), Queens is its major hinge. A dozen satellite Chinatowns and "Little Manilas," "Little Seouls," along with our modest "Little Delhi" cluster around the "el" tracks of Elmhurst, Corona, Flushing, and Long Island City, and "Little Bogota" at the Junction Boulevard end of Jackson Heights. This is the story of just one New America, that of Indian, Pakistani, Bangladeshi and Sri Lankan immigrants. In the New World of Queens, the old intact India, dismembered since 1947, reconstitutes itself every weekend in the jewelry stores and restaurants, the 220-volt appliance stores and Hindi/Urdu video rentals and spice shops of Jackson Heights.

The two-block core, north from the 74th Street station, really doesn't add up to much. This is no cluttered, twisting Chinatown, no fetid, reconstructed Bombay *chowk*. As in many Asian societies, the street presents a far more modest aspect than the reality behind it. This is the commercial heart of New York's prosperous Indian community, yet it is still, recognizably, one kind of a Queens street, with its three-story semi-detached frame and brick homes. Only the ground floors have been converted—with a minimum of effort and expense —for commercial use. It's Queens much the way the departing Greeks and Italians left it, on their way further out to Long Island.

No familiar chain stores in evidence. Mom and pop, you might think, remembering Mario Cuomo's father in his grocery store, remembering Morris Bober in Bernard Malamud's *The Assistant*. A new generation, hustling a modest living. Yes and No. They are all moms and pops, and their hustle nearly redeems the good name of greed, but the modest storefronts are tips of commercial icebergs.

Back in India, "74th Street" is a legend. This is the New York street India knows, the equivalent of all those Hester Streets, Grand Concourses and Flatbushes of other immigrant waves. It's where visiting honeymooners have their pictures taken, where Indian-made films are shot, where visitors from India stock up on goods they can't find, or afford, back home, and where American-resident Indians buy their going-home gifts. To own a shop on 74th Street is to have a niche at the gaming table: a guaranteed clientele with money and the cul-turally-stamped imperatives for buying gifts—major gifts—for every relative, on every trip back home.

These are chain stores, linked with Vancouver, Toronto, Los Angeles, Atlanta, Boston, Chicago, London. The Internat-ional Sari Palace (ISP) is a franchise operation, run out of Hong Kong. Patel Brothers, the spice shop, is a chain with eight-een outlets. Sam & Raj, the appliance store, a fixture on the block since 1973, is a major transferer of American video tapes for Indian VCRs—it's practically a major studio—as well as the biggest exporter of 220-volt appliances in the country. In In-dia they say, "Go to America. Go to the Statue of Liberty. Go to Sam & Raj." And do they ever visit! Five- to ten thou-sand every summer weekend. There's a major Indian movie producer on 74th Street, Kanu Chauhan, CEO of ten corpor-ations, owner or developer of most of the businesses on 74th Street, but known to Americans only as the head of a Century 21 agency. The Jackson Diner, Indian to the core despite its name, serves 500 meals a day at the diner, and another 125, on the average, at weddings, conferences, religious feasts, all over the Tri-State area.

Little India is a commercial gold mine because it caters to Indian cultural tastes. Religious rituals inevitably involve food and gifts. Travel—and this is a traveling community, in balance with India, still in intimate contact with parents and siblings "over there"—demands as great an investment in gifts as it does in airfare. If, for example, an Indian professional living in New Jersey, upstate New York, southern Connecticut or eastern Pennsylvania, has a daughter to marry, who's he going to call? He can rent a local hall, of course, but what about the music, the gods, the food, the priests, the gifts?

Suddenly, 74th Street becomes the longest street in Amer-ica. It stretches. Everything in India is elastic, including its sat-ellite culture in America. Call the Lord Ganapati Temple in Flushing. (While you're at it, call up Jackson Diner for cater-ing. Go to ISP for gift-saris. Rent a weekend's slate of Hindi movies. Buy your guests thoughtful appliances at Sam & Raj.) The Temple can dispatch as many India-trained swamis as you're likely to need.

"Rent-a-Swami?" we ask, only partially amazed. "One of our biggest money-makers," the Temple Executive Director, former Air-India controller, Mr. Ram Chandran chuckles. Of course there are pieties in Hindu devotion, which one dares not interrupt. Chanting clusters of worshippers arrange themselves in front of each garlanded god, reciting Sanskrit mantras by the hour. But Temple management, with its board of directors, its architects and workers and its cartons of milk and bowls of fruit, and robed swamis shopping at the local convenience stores, is devotional housekeeping, eminently level-headed.

Shopping in Indian areas is a form of theater-going, a rite of permanent celebration. On weekends, entire three- and four-generation families inspect the sari shops, stop in for lunch, stock up on spices. Men accompany their wives to sari shops in India, and here; sari-shopping is family-business. The families may look Americanized, especially the teenagers, but this Queens community, as opposed to longer-established suburban or New Jersey residents, is fairly recently-arrived, still in transition. They have come to America, generally, under provisions of family reunification, not for their invaluable professional talent. America is still a little alien, India a comfort.

The ability to preserve the culture—language, worship, food, clothing—is a matter of universal pride among Indians, challenged now by American openness and affluence. (It used to be said that an Indian immigrant with a twelve-year-old daughter was under enormous pressure to pull up stakes and return. The prospect of not being able to arrange her marriage, or worse, being defied, was too shameful to contemplate. Now the community is large enough to socialize, and marry, within.) Preservation of culture requires a commercial network, with foods, films, saris, and temple, all at hand. Indian immigrants are often cited as a "model community," making more money, and saving it more efficiently than they ever could in India, but they have nowhere to spend it, except on airfare home, college tuition, and in the familiar shops of 74th Street. Their entertainment is centered on the family, on the rental of Hindi (or Urdu, or other regional-language) movies, on watching the three New-York-based, India- or Pakistani-based television networks, which offer local amateur talent, community bulletin boards, interviews, ads, movies, news and film clips from overseas.

The major singers and film stars of India and Pakistan are in a continual shuttle between Bombay, London, New York, Toronto and Los Angeles, selling-out major auditoria, hosting-benefits, and opening community events. There's even a nation-wide "Miss Indo-American Beauty Contest," staged in New York, MC'd by a Bombay superstar, sponsored by a consortium of America-based Indian companies, where all those assimilated suburban Indian girls get a chance to show off their dancing and singing, and their comportment, in dress and sari. The winners are usually "good girls" in saris who do traditional indian dance, but the whistles and applause go to those perfectly assimilated, long-legged beauties in bodysuits who opt for interpretive jazzercise.

You want to aim for a good Indian lunch, a south Indian *dosa* (thin lentil batter crepe, folded like a giant funnel and stuffed with spiced potato) at Udipi, or any of Jackson Diner's excellent curries or tandooris. Go early and work up an appetite. Of course, Indian-food lovers hardly need to work up anything; the aroma, and the sight of twenty tables occupied by Indian families dipping food with their fingers awakens the gastronome in anyone.

Arrive early, have a curry at the Jackson Diner, or a *dosa* at Udipi, some sweets at Shaheen's, inspect the silks at ISP or across the street at Krishna Sari Center, the gold jewelry at Bhimji's, stop in a spice store and buy a burlap sack of *basmati* rice, a plastic bag of frozen *naan* bread, some "Hot Mix" to go with beer and ballgames. Bring a decent Indian cookbook, Madhur Jaffray's, say, and check the recipes. Stock up on spices unavailable anywhere else. Ask anyone for help, but be prepared for a long, historical and cultural response. You're in an older culture now, chaotic with children and lack of automation, but aromatic enough to keep you rooted. You're in a place where, like Ben Jonson's Sir Epicure Mammon in *The Alchemist*, you can "dream your meat in Indian shells, the tongues of carps, dormice, and camel's heels, boiled in the spirit of Sol and dissolved pearl."

With the time remaining, get back on the subway, out past Shea Stadium to Main Street Flushing. Take a bus to 45-57 Bowne Street and walk around, then inspect one of New York's strangest architectural wonders: a vast, utterly authentic Temple, half a block of south India duplicated intact, as improbable as The Sphinx, and dropped in Archie Bunker's Queens. The Temple richly explains itself in its own brochures, but it welcomes questions. Its architecture, inside and out, its nineteen-year financial history is an epic, starting with $51 ("the sacred number of Lord Skanda") and standing now at an evaluation of several million. For $61,000 they bought a Russian Orthodox church that was on the block for $100,000, razed it, and built the Ganapati Temple, with stone masons from India and the financial assistance of the Andhra Pradesh state government. This is an enormous undertaking: the black granite sanctum of Lord Gahapati weighs fifty tons; all temple carving required 220 tons. Gradually, the Temple has bought every house on the block, starting when they cost $15,000 apiece, now at twenty times that amount. All of this is attributable, according to the director, to specific instructions received in dreams from the legendary Sage Agastya, founder of the Tamil language, guru of all the sages, that Lord Ganesha wanted his abode in a city whose name began with the letter "N". This proved providential, even obliging, given that the petitioners were living in New York City. As a practical convenience, it had also to be within a one-fare public transportation zone to the majority of worshippers. The Temple is open to all, provided they take off their shoes.

We're sitting in the Jackson Diner on the corner of 74th Street and 37th Avenue, talking with the owner, "Bobby" Chhikara. He's a tall, engaging, athletic man with short hair and boyish features. The Jackson Diner looks like a diner ("a real rutputty joint," Salman Rushdie described a similar authentic Bombay hangout in *Midnight's Children*), with its green plastic decor trimmed in chrome, and fluorescent lighting. It has always been a diner, but it does not serve diner food. The Jackson Diner is Jackson Heights' premier Indian restaurant. We are eating a plate of samosas, dipping them in mint chutney, and sipping spiced tea. Lunches (non-vegetarian or vegetarian) go for about four dollars, dinners for under seven. Asked to recommend his own best entrees, he suggests boti kabob and makhani chicken.

Bobby is relating the tale of his eventful life, how a boy from a hill village in Haryana won a scholarship to military school, suffered a boxing injury, and was declared unfit for military service. "Trust God," he says now. A friend steered him to hotel management ("I thought, 'Oh, boy, everyone's dressed up. This is the life for me'," he tells us now), where he trained, eventually mastering pastries, wine, and western cooking.

In 1981 he arrived in Queens, and bought a small Greek diner on installment. He kept the German and Argentine waiters, who simply developed a new expertise. He learned American management skills. ("I pushed too hard in India. Here, you can't do that. A man makes 900 *naan* a day, you have to find ways of motivating him, not just ordering him about.") For a couple of years he served more pasta and lamb than Indian food, got up at four o'clock to serve breakfast. Then he expanded from fifty seats to seventy, developed the catering service, moved entirely to Indian, cut out breakfasts, and *still*

kept a majority non-Indian clientele during the week. He gross-
es now, more than five times the purchase price.

The point is, he is a professional, professionally trained in
India in every manner of European and Asian cuisine, in pastries, in wines, before immigrating. This is a major success story:
village-born boy wins scholarship, suffers reversal, discovers
hotel management, food servicing, and the rest, and in less than
ten years of hard, stolid, immigrant labor, he is owner of a 74th
Street landmark. His wife is Trinidad-Indian; the village boy
who spoke no English until he won a scholarship now is forced
to speak English in every aspect of his life. His life is lived entirely in America.

Just above the Diner hangs a Century 21 sign. Rajsun Real-
ties, with its forty agents, is one of the companies of Mr. Kanu
Chauhan, the man most responsible for the commercial devel-
opment of 74th Street. Mr. Chauhan's ten corporations in India and America are all titled "Rajsun," a compound made of
his two sons' names. We meet him in his office one night, long
after hours. He calls downstairs for a plate of somosas and tea.
The phones keep ringing, an architect arrives with plans; we
inspect the Hindi film posters on his wall, wondering exactly
why they're there. Had we known where to look, we would
have seen the Rajsun Productions logo.

Like Bobby of the Diner, Chauhan is a village boy, with an
engineering degree, from Gujarat. His talent is for making
money, and talking with him, we appreciate how like a gift, a
special talent, it is. He came to the United States in 1970, to
Brooklyn, opened a grocery store and sold it at a profit; opened an Indian restaurant in Manhattan and sold it a year later
at an enormous profit, then had a revelation: buying and selling is the fastest way of making money, and real estate is the
epitome of that kind of money-making. He came to 74th
Street, the first Indian realtor, the second Indian after Sam &
Raj, because prices were low and the Greeks and Italians were
anxious to sell and move further out to Long Island. The Chinese and Koreans and Indians were moving in.

Prices were rising steadily, and sometimes spectacularly, for fifteen years. Ten-thousand-dollar investments in rental properties, made by immigrants earning $250 a week, had grown to half-million-dollar properties. If there is a thread to the stories we've heard, and not just from Mr. Chauhan, it's the steadiness, the inevitability of the climb to wealth. All goals have been met, ahead of schedule. Occasional setbacks are viewed as revelation, like Bobby Chhikara's boxing injury. Nothing is permanently lost; everything can be turned to gain. No wonder immigrants can sometimes be hated.

If the story ended there, Kanu Chauhan would seem two-dimensional: driven, disciplined, shrewd, saving. Lucky—but essentially bloodless. But Kanu Chauhan, the man of many corporations, is a multi-sided figure. In America he speaks with a thick accent and wears three-piece suits, and designs new shopping malls for 74th Street. In India, where he is featured in Hindi film magazines as an overseas producer, he wears open-necked shirts and aviator sun glasses. Film stars blossom on each arm. He keeps an office and home on Bombay's Juhu Beach (India's Malibu). His first film, "Jaaydaad," meaning (what else?) "Real Estate," was released this spring.

Movie making is his passion. He wanted to be an actor in India, but came to America instead. Fate: it has made him a wealthy man. Now comes indulgence: film. He is a man deeply rooted in both countries. In fact, he is almost two separate men. No one would connect the sober Queens businessman with the jaunty young producer. He plans to make six more Hindi films, then start producing American films.

"Pure American film," he tells us, and we know he's not talking of Merchant and Ivory here, or Satyajit Ray. "Rambo," he grins, and there he sits before us in his office with the posters, the plate of crumbly samosa shells, the tea cups: Sam Goldwyn of a different time and place.

Bobby calls us one night and says, "a friend is here at the diner. He just came back from India. He's very special, and I think you should talk to him." He has just won the bronze medal in the Culinary Olympics, in Switzerland.

And so we visit, at his invitation, for a Saturday brunch, in his third-floor apartment across Broadway on a street of Korean offices. His name is Chris Jaswani and he is the executive sous-chef of the Chase Manhattan kitchen. Back in New Delhi, Bobby had been his instructor in the school of hotel management.

We close on Chris ("Chitranjan was hard to pronounce, Chris is easier. Changing my name doesn't change my heart, my feelings, or the way I am; it just makes it easier for people.") and on the memories of a lunch that made us into Epicure Mammons ("... calvered salmons, the beards of barbels served instead of salads; oiled mushrooms; and the swelling unctuous paps of a fat, pregnant sow, newly cut off..."), because he arises, *unpredictably* from the same community of model immigrants, but is an aesthetic and sensual genius; not a businessman, not a producer.

The walls are hung with pictures, but they are pictures of dishes he's created. Arranged on white plates, they seem at first modernist paintings. He grew up in an artistic home in Delhi. "I became a cook," he tells us from the kitchen where he's making the first of a five-course brunch, "when my mother wouldn't let me into the kitchen. When she gave me clothing money, I saved until I could buy *Larousse Gastronomique*. Somehow I could imagine what those recipes would look like, and taste like, even though I was a vegetarian in India. I see a recipe once, and I retain it. (He is writing a vegetarian cookbook for Van Nostrand, due out in 1990.) I use the subway trip to Manhattan to think about my recipes; by the time I get to the Chase Tower, I've created something special." He shows us one: mako shark with lichee nut sauce. The shark was rolled with a filling of tofu, lobster, sushi rice and nasturtium petals, then grilled.

"I wanted to serve people," he goes on. His sisters and mother didn't love to cook—he finally convinced them to let him try. He's serving us now: an American omelette. Then Chinese noodles and lamb. French. Japanese. He sits and critiques his own food—too much salt in the marrow-stock. He remembers his first training at the Taj Hotel—"Bobby taught me Beef Stroganoff"—but then he went on to Zurich, France, Germany, before taking more training at the Culinary Institute of America, then taking over kitchens in California. Eventually, he would like to open a perfect restaurant, in Forest Hills, Queens. Not Indian.

He is Indian, of course, but in other ways, not Indian at all. He springs from a concept more Western than Indian, but he brings to his cooking the keen pleasure that Indians take in other people's pleasure. "Indian cooking is so repetitive," he confides. "Same basic spices, same basic foods, cooked the same basic way. You are not encouraged to be creative."

Unyielding consistency, of course, is part of India; its pride in continuity and stability. For an artist, for the children of Queens who will have to face the varieties of American experience, rather than the certainties of an Indian life in which everything is predictable and laid out from birth to death, for a sophisticate like Chris, and for us, the need to preserve the culture intact, in all its aspects, would be stifling. Every recipe that Chris reads inspires a variation; culinary jazz. He dares to break the rules.

Immigrant jazz. Theme and variation.

America is singing in all these Little Bombays and Seouls and Manilas. Take an eating and shopping and people-watching stroll down 74th Street. What you see is not always all there is. Perhaps, in immigration, it never is.

Joseph Barbato
IN SEARCH OF THE NEW AMERICA
Notes for a Work in Progress

Wednesday, May 23, 1990

Yesterday, Joey asked me, "Am I Italian, Dad?" I said yes, that since my father's parents came from Italy, and we have an Italian name, he can call himself Italian. This morning, he announces that he is an American. His teacher, Mrs. Zavlek, is counting him that way because he is third-generation. That makes Joey the only American among the thirty-three pupils in his fourth-grade class at P.S. 89. His classmates' families are recent immigrants from Peru, Honduras, Trinidad, Puerto Rico, Poland, China, Taiwan, Korea, India, Thailand, the Philippines, and Iraq. Nine are of mixed descent, meaning their parents were born in different countries.

"Everyone else comes from a foreign-born family?" I ask.

"Except for Michael, he's only from Iraq," says Joey. Michael lives down the block. He and George, whose family is from Yugoslavia, are Joey's closest friends.

"Joey, Iraq is halfway around the world," I reply. Joey, who is ten, doesn't respond. To him, Michael must seem like an American. Except on days when they've vowed not to be friends anymore, Joey and Michael hang out together. They belong to the same Cub Scout pack and bowling league. In a neighborhood where most people speak Spanish or an Asian tongue, Michael's family talks Armenian at home, which makes Michael different, just like Joey.

We live in Elmhurst, Queens, the most ethnically diverse neighborhood in New York City. Our neighbors come from 120 countries and speak forty languages. Elmhurst is an ordinary, working-class area, occupying about one and a quarter square miles of western Queens and little-noticed in the glitzy flow of New York life. Each morning on the radio, commuter traffic reports mention the Elmhurst tanks ("Delays of up to fifteen minutes at the Elmhurst tanks . . ."), familiar guideposts on the Long Island Expressway. Whenever a plane crashes at

LaGuardia Airport, the evening news includes interviews with survivors brought to Elmhurst Hospital. Elmhurst is a backdrop for the news, rarely news itself.

Yet Elmhurst is an early glimpse into the American future. By the year 2100, according to the Census Bureau, the population of the United States will be ten percent Asian, seventeen percent black, twenty-seven percent Hispanic, and forty-six percent white. For the first time, whites will be a minority in a multicultural America.

Elmhurst is there now. Only forty percent of its more than 75,000 residents are white. The majority of the population is Hispanic (thirty-six percent), Asian (twenty-two percent), and black (about two percent). They include people we have known for years: Mario and his father, mother and sister, a Peruvian family that I first met while waiting for Joey's kindergarten bus; Nancy Hsu, an indefatigable Chinese woman who leads the Elmhurst Girl Scouts; my daughter's friends Poonam and Pornima Tavkar, from India, and Darlene Perry, from Trinidad; and the Kims, a Korean couple across the street, who work late into the night in their Brooklyn laundromat, and whose kids, Jenny and Jimmy, often play at our house and wind up staying for dinner.

Who are these immigrants from the Third World who have transformed my neighborhood? Why do they come? At what risk? What was life like for them in their home countries? What's it like here?

It is not as if I have never pondered such questions during my years in Elmhurst. My work and interests have simply taken me elsewhere. Yet inexorably, month by month and year by year, I'd notice the increasing diversity of my neighbors' ethnicity. Imagine living in a community so dominated by immigrants that another parent asks you at an open-school night, "And what country are you from?" I almost said America. In truth, I can't remember what I blurted, probably something about being born here.

I was curious about my neighbors—but how to act on my

curiosity? Many adult immigrants do not speak English. Even when they do, might they not be understandably suspicious of questions about their lives? Who was I to ask why they were in Elmhurst? So I went about my business, saying the few words that needed saying when dealing with the Indian man at the newsstand, the Filipino doctor who cares for our kids, the Hispanic girls at the coffee shop, and the Chinese lady at the bakery. It's a truism: New Yorkers never know their neighbors.

When I learned that the Ford Foundation and the National Science Foundation were studying my neighborhood as a precursor of the American city of the future, I felt like the neighbor asked to comment about the serial killer just arrested next door: "He was a quiet, polite guy—never gave anybody any trouble." That, I realized, was the level of my insight into my neighbors in Elmhurst, Queens. I lived in the community, but I was not *of* it. I did not know my neighbors, and they did not know me. Somehow, in that not-knowing, we got along.

And that was the most remarkable thing about Elmhurst. It included people from a mind-boggling array of ethnicities and skin colors, it was the American future, and it worked. For reasons that social scientists were just beginning to discover— the healing role of ethnic churches, the coming together over shared concerns such as drugs and crime—there was a relative harmony in Elmhurst.

We certainly did not have the racial and ethnic conflict so evident elsewhere. In the Flatbush section of Brooklyn, blacks and Koreans were clashing over an incident involving a black Haitian woman and a Korean greengrocer. In Bensonhurst, African-Americans marched through the streets in protest over the 1989 killing there of Yusuf Hawkins, a black teenager; some whites, mainly Italian-Americans like the slain youth's accused assailants, shouted racial epithets from the sidewalks. Elsewhere in the country, even on college campuses—especially on campuses, which with their increasingly mixed student bodies have become testing grounds in multicultural living—

there were signs of problems ahead for the new America in the making. In Baltimore, the National Institute Against Prejudice and Violence issued a report detailing incidents of "ethnoviolence" at more than 300 colleges since 1986. At Wesleyan University, racial slurs were found spray-painted on the walls of a black cultural center. At the University of Georgia, eggs were thrown through the dormitory window of a student from Singapore. "We are in for a few years of ethnic and racial turmoil," said the director of the Institute for the Study of Social Change at the University of California at Berkeley.

In the past, I had watched with amusement as culturally aware New Yorkers indulged themselves in a superficial acquaintance with my neighborhood. On one occasion, Manhattan's 92nd Street Y had offered a walking tour of Elmhurst, so that day-trippers could see such phenomena as a funeral home turned Korean church, and dine on Thai food at the Jaiya Restaurant across the street from my apartment, or on lomo relleno (stuffed pork) or lengua en salsa (stewed beef tongue) at Restaurant Sur America, one of the city's oldest Colombian restaurants, around the corner. Neighborhood food shops and bakeries, such as La Sorpresa, noted for its Colombian breads and snacks, had become a staple of the food pages of *The New York Times*. It all smacked of slumming to me.

Then the *Newsday* columnist Jimmy Breslin made his unfortunate remarks. A young colleague, a Korean-American woman working out of the paper's Queens bureau, had criticized a Breslin column as sexist. Infuriated, Breslin let loose a vituperative bevy of obscenity and racial slurs. A "yellow cur," he called her. This from the Breslin, himself a Queens native, whose work I so admired. The Breslin with whom I once spent an afternoon on the streets of the south Bronx, where young Hispanic kids ran up to greet him. The Breslin who used to hang out at the Liffey Bar in Elmhurst, a few blocks from my apartment. The Breslin who knew better.

More troubling than my disappointment in Breslin was my disappointment in myself. For I understood his anger. I understood it at each of its levels. First, a Pulitzer winner, a pro's pro, he had been attacked by a young whippersnapper—a twenty-five-year-old out in the Queens office, for God's sake. Second, she was a foreigner, as good a category of the other as any. As will happen, Breslin reached from his initial anger to the latent level where each of us finds mud to sling at those who are different.

It was a monumental loss of temper. Or was it? Breslin trades on fierce honesty, and there is in his work the tension of opposites. The streetwise intellectual, he is also a bit of the good old boy. Each persona keeps the other in check. That day, he was pure redneck. In a moment's rage, a man who could tell you about signs that once read NO IRISH NEED APPLY, hung out his own sign that said, in effect, KEEP YOUR ASIAN MOUTH SHUT.

Immigrants are different. My father's father spoke only Italian, smoked smelly cigars, grew fig trees in his backyard, and read *Il Progresso* daily. I think of him often now when I walk the streets of Elmhurst. In a foul mood, I am easily annoyed by the behavior of my neighbors: A group of young Hispanics hanging out on a streetcorner and ogling young women. Asian women babbling in loud voices. The snooty-seeming attitude of an Indian storekeeper. A foreign-born woman—her nationality uncertain and irrelevant—sneaking ahead at the supermarket checkout. I cringe when, in this latter sort of situation, a white shopper snarls, "Why don't you people go back where you came from?" Or when another white, miffed over a perceived slight, shouts, "What's that you say? I don't understand you. My language is English. That's what we talk here." I am polite and educated. I would never talk like that. Would I?

Are we threatened by the new immigrants? Are we put off by their thirld world customs, religions, and manners? By the refusal of some to assimilate totally to American ways?

Although they are my neighbors in Elmhurst. I confess that I don't know these immigrants. Why are they here? What are their hopes and dreams and heartbreaks? What are their stories?

How is it that they have been able to live together—with dozens of other new immigrant groups as well as with whites of European descent—in relative harmony? What can they tell us about their past and present that will help us to better understand and prepare for our country's future? And what of Elmhurst's white old-timers—Americans who now comprise the new group that sociologist Richard D. Alba of the State University of New York at Albany, calls the "European Americans"? What are their attitudes toward the newcomers from Asia, Latin America and the Caribbean?

Even as I set out to find the answers to such questions, I realize that the matter has urgency in this period of racial and ethnic turmoil. We can no longer remain ignorant of these new immigrants, for it is out of ignorance that suspicion and stereotyping arise. Ignorance, or worse, a simplistic tabloid-headline understanding, leads to talk about Koreans arriving here with paper bags brimming with cash, and Colombians jaunting about in big cars bought with cocaine profits. Behind the barriers—the lack of English, the smelly cigars, and the foreign-language newspapers—there stands somebody's grandfather.

For more than twenty years, Elmhurst has been my neighborhood. It never seemed unusual, perhaps because my wife and I have lived in Queens all our lives. We'd walked these streets as kids growing up close by in Jackson Heights in the 1950s, gone to Saturday double features at the Jackson and Elmwood movie houses, visited ailing relatives at Elmhurst Hospital. Maybe we were more open-minded than other whites. Was that it? My wife had become a teacher of English as a second language, and taught immigrant children in a Queens public school every day. Many of her former students lived in our neighborhood. As for me, like many New Yorkers in the outer boroughs, my neighborhood was simply the bedroom to which I returned from a day's work in Manhattan. Over the years, salaried jobs brought me to offices in Rockefeller Center, the Village, and the upper East Side. That was the real New York. At night, I would ride the subway home to Elmhurst, at once safe and predictable even as it became more foreign.

We moved to Elmhurst in the late 1960s, and I can still recall my mother remarking, "Why, it's like a little U.N.," when
she saw the tenant directory in the lobby of our new apartment building. Latin Americans, mainly Colombians, were just
beginning to move in. Many residents were German- and
French- and Italian-Americans. Most of the storefronts on
Broadway, a main shopping street, had English-language signs.
There was an Irish bar, a Jewish deli, and an old-fashioned
German-American restaurant called The Hofbrau. Koreans
own the deli now. The other stores—the candy story, the ice
cream shop, the European tailor—are gone. They have been replaced by Queens Oriental Food and Gifts, Zam-Zam Halal
Meats, Komdar Sari, Foods of India of Elmhurst, Latino Travel Agency, Yi Mei Bakery, and Botay Hairstylist. The Hofbrau, which my wife and I, then childless young marrieds,
thought quite elegant, caught fire one night in the '70s. Two
dozen fire trucks responded to the alarm. The burning restaurant was next door to our building, but my wife and I slept
quietly the whole night. We awoke to the sight of trucks and
hoses and the charred remnants of what had been.

The U.S. Post Office at Elmhurst now stands on the site of
the old Hofbrau. It must be one of the most unusual post offices in the United States. Each morning at 8:30, men and
women line up with packages addressed to cities and villages
in India, Ecuador, the Philippines, and other countries. Sometimes they come in twos, and you will hear the sounds of Spanish, Indian, or a Chinese dialect. But generally the crowded
little postal lobby is quiet, except for the cries of some child,
or the complaints in unaccented English of a long-time neighborhood resident upset over the long wait and the failure to
provide more postal clerks. The postal station makes no con-
cession to foreign-born patrons. Its signs, describing overnight
mail services, or new stamps commemorating Babe Ruth and
Ernest Hemingway, are in English—the one thing the lack of
which unites these dozens of men and women with their par-

cels of clothing, money and other items destined for home countries, even as it enforces the near total silence among them. Now and then a clerk will call out, "Does anyone here speak Chinese?" Or, "Is anyone from the Philippines?" Once, an Asian man on line ahead of me went up to help an Asian woman who was having trouble communicating at the clerk's window. They exchanged a few words, and the man quickly returned to his place with an embarrassed smile. He apparently spoke the wrong language, or the wrong dialect of the woman's language. In this room where English was the working tongue, one Asian could not talk to another.

Today is the day of the annual International Day Parade at Joey's school. Ethnic celebrations are held throughout the year in Elmhurst, but only P.S. 89's parade brings all of the residents together. Parents, grandparents, and others crowd the sidewalks in front of the school. P.S. 89 is the elementary school for most Elmhurst children. In another era its pupils came from Polish, German, Italian, Irish and eastern European Jewish families. Now they speak forty languages and have surnames like Garcia and Gutierrez, and Ng, Sen, Yo, Lim and Koo. Many attend bilingual classes. Some take lessons in broomclosets that were converted into classrooms. Like many New York public schools, P.S. 89 is overcrowded. Three new schools are planned for the school district, and they will be at one-hundred percent utilization the day they open. Such is the price paid for the neglect of city officials, who ignored the rapid growth of Elmhurst's school-age population in the 1970s and '80s, and were under no pressure to do otherwise, from an immigrant community without political clout.

None of this matters today. The morning air is crisp, the sky a canopy of pastel-blue. The onlookers have double-checked their cameras and seized places behind police stanchions. They are women, mostly: thirty-ish Indians in saris, elderly Chinese, young Hispanics in sale-store t-shirts and too much makeup. Pride and hope cry out from their faces. For days the children of P.S. 89 have been preparing costumes and rehearsing dances.

The color guard of four children steps forward in the middle of the street, bearing the American, state, city and school flags. Joey is one of them. The others are Tyrik Mack, Roxann Peniche and George Ormond. Joey is wearing my old vest, and I recall our frantic phone-calling of the night before. Each boy in Joey's fourth-grade class needed a vest to wear in the dance they will do today. Kris Kingpayom didn't have a vest, so Joey loaned him his sister's. But the vest was too big, and when Joey got home yesterday he said Kris's mother was going to cut the vest down to size. My wife was furious: "You gave him permission to do that without talking to me!" So we had to call Kris's house fast, before the thirty-dollar vest was destroyed. Joey didn't have Kris's phone number, nor did any of his friends. We turned to the Queens phone book and found several dozen entries under "Kingpayon," many in Elmhurst. This went on for half an hour, with my wife calling out the numbers of all the Elmhurst Kingpayons, and Joey dialing. "Is Kris there? Is Kris there?" No Kris. So the question remained: has Kris's mother done the unthinkable?

An assistant principal leads in the Pledge of Allegiance, and then the "Star Spangled Banner" echoes along the street from a PA system. I fight back tears. I feel a surge within. I suppose it is adrenalin coursing in the blood. I feel as if I want to catch my breath. It is a moment of warmth and grace. I can only guess at its meaning for each man and woman here.

While "Stars and Stripes Forever" plays, the children begin marching, one class after another, through the neighborhood. Some hold brightly colored signs: "We Are All the Same." "The World Is Home to Us All." Many wear the clothing of their homelands, or of other nations whose dances they will perform after completing the parade route. Three Korean women carry a sign: "We Love All."

Usually I watch this parade from the sidelines, but today I join in. From the front, behind a police van that leads the way, I see the excitement of residents watching from stoops and apartment windows as we move down Britton Avenue toward Broadway. Two young Hispanic women and an older woman with a baby in her arms smile from a doorway. Workmen watch from scaffolding around a three-family home under construction. On a balcony opposite, an Asian woman in a yellow nightgown notices my upward gaze. She ducks behind a curtain and peers around it.

These are the streets of the new Elmhurst. They are not so unlike the opening pan of homes in the television series "All in the Family," which was set in Queens and featured a real-life Elmhurst boy, Carroll O'Connor, as America's favorite bigot, Archie Bunker. As it happens, O'Connor grew up on this very street. From the ages of four to nine, he lived with his family in a four-story walk-up at 87-15 Britton Avenue, three blocks from his classes at P.S. 89. His childhood Elmhurst of the late 1920s and early '30s was quiet and quasi-rural, with many truck farms. In the post-World War II baby boom, the area filled with row houses. There are still many in the area, interspersed with six-story low-rises and three-story brick homes built in the 1970s and '80s to accommodate the influx of third world immigrants.

Except for faces on the street, you would have little reason to think that this is an immigrant neighborhood. After several blocks, just as the procession is about to turn right onto Layton Avenue, I notice a sign in Chinese characters in a house window. It may advertise day care, a car for sale, or for all I know, church services. From this corner we can see the Clement Clarke Moore Homestead Park, a block away on Broadway, where I used to push Louise and Joey on swings. In the early mornings, elderly Chinese come there to do Tai Chi. Throughout the day the city park is packed with parents, children and a complement of derelicts and drug users. In the nineteenth century, in his ancestral home there, Dr. Moore wrote "'Twas the Night Before Christmas," an occasion commemorated each Christmas Eve with a tree-lighting, and caroling by a Korean chorus.

The children march two blocks down Layton and turn right on Pettit Avenue, which will bring them back toward P.S. 89. This is now the route our kids have followed each day to get to school from our apartment on the corner. Further up Layton, a giant crane looms above the visible portion of the 792-bed City Hospital Center at Elmhurst, whose emergency room is one of the busiest in the city, with more than 100,000 visits each year. Most patients are from the community, and the hospital has volunteers who can assist in more than sixty languages. Demands on the hospital's facilities have prompted a hundred million dollar renovation.

Along Pettit, we pass shingles hung out by immigrant dentists and doctors, a common sight in a community that offers services of every description for each ethnic group, from Chinese acupuncture to Indian video rentals. Again, row houses here and there have given way to the ubiquitous three-story brick homes, many with relatives from the same family (aunts, uncles, grandparents) living on different floors and contributing to mortgages. From Pettit, the parade turns right into Ithaca Street, which takes us back to the school.

Now the dancing begins: The Charleston and the Shoo Fly. The Korean Puppet Dance, and Indian and Chinese dances. The Conga. The Irish Washerwoman, and more. Joey's class does the Hustle: "Do the Hustle! Get down!" I watch him and how uncharacteristically serious he is, intent on getting his steps just right. It's a big day for these kids, and there's lots more ahead: international food-tastings in their classrooms, with dishes their parents have brought in this morning.

Later my wife and I will visit Joey's class and learn Kris's mother has not altered Louise's vest but used another. Some of the kids will remember me from the trip to the Museum of Modern Art that I went on with them weeks before. An Indian girl will sit across from me and smile, remarking knowingly as we eat, "Joey has a crush on Norell. All the boys do." Just then, the boys will be far more interested in their Gameboys and portable radios—special dispensations of International Day

—than with the class femme fatale.

My wife's lasagna, our "Italian" contribution to the luncheon, will disappear quickly. It always does on International Day. It once prompted a teacher to remark, "American food! Thank God!" The kids seem to feel that way too. This year, a Chinese first-grader complained in an essay that his parents eat only ethnic food. "When we eat outside, we have a big problem!" he wrote. "I want to go to McDonald's, but my mom and dad don't want to, so we always bring a hamburger into the Chinese restaurant where my parents like to eat."

Not many parents will come up to the classroom today. Most work, and others do not speak English. We will chat politely with those who come, but language will be a problem. It always is. But not for the children of P.S. 89. For the parents and others who lined Britton Avenue this morning, they represent the future. You do not have to hear the children talking for long—these children from throughout Asia and Latin America—to know that that future is decidedly American. They are fluent in English. They know what's happening at the Simpsons', the latest songs by the New Kids on the Block, and the price of a burger and fries at McDonald's on Queens Boulevard.

Yet, at home when the school day is over—what then? I know that Joey's friend Michael goes to Armenian school, and that Jenny Kim and her family go to a Korean church each Sunday in Flushing, where there is a large Korean community. What do their parents want for them? And what of their parents and grandparents? What is life like for them in Elmhurst? How do they view neighbors from other immigrant groups, and the white minority from European backgrounds? How, finally, do they account for the racial and ethnic harmony of Elmhurst?

For there is no question that while discord and strife elsewhere in New York City captivate the attention of the nation, Elmhurst, a yeasty multicultural stew of 120 ethnic groups, is peaceful. Yet even now, as the last class of children performs on Britton Avenue, and the P.S. 89 principal, Cleonice LoSecco, takes the microphone, no one seems to notice the hopeful calm in this most ethnically diverse of all the city's neighborhoods.

"Our mayor and all of the leaders of our city have been asking for racial peace," she tells the throng gathered this International Day. "We at P.S. 89 have had racial peace for many years. We *have* the 'gorgeous mosaic'."

Salimah Ali, photographer

Salimah Ali, photographer

FOLLOWING THE THREAD

Edited by Lisa Weinerman Horak

America is not like a blanket of one piece of unbroken cloth, one color, one texture; America is more like a quilt—many pieces of many sizes, many colors, and held together by a common thread. —Jesse Jackson

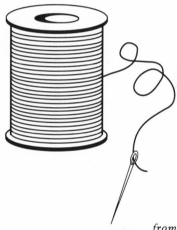

NORMAN CLARKE

My first eight years were spent growing up in post-war London, learning about America twice a week in the twilight aisles of the local cinema, taught by John Wayne.

Now we were in the real America. Not John Wayne's wild west but just as different. Just how different was never more evident, never more clear than on our first Christmas shopping trip.

The sidewalks of Steinway Street were a bustling mass of individuality kept within its bounds only by the mountains of snow piled at the curbside. Bathed in flashing lights we joined this caravan of window shoppers gathered from all parts of the earth, sloshing along past German bakeries, Italian delicatessens, Irish taverns and countless Greek restaurants, each step unveiling a newer, more delicious smell, each window a more enticing sight. Things could not have been more different, more fantastic to me if I had wandered into a bazaar in Arabia.

DANIEL T. SCHWEIKERT

In those days, neighborhoods throughout the city were generally made up of one dominant ethnic group. This was the obvious result of immigrants following relatives and friends to America. Where there was more than one, the other group, or groups, usually lived in enclaves within the neighborhood of the dominant nationality, thereby maintaining their own ethnic identity. And there was yet a third situation where, although one group dominated a neighborhood by sheer weight of numbers, people of other nationalities lived side by side and among the major ethnic group.

Middle Village was of this third type. Although people of German extraction were in the majority, we had many Irish, some Italians, Poles and other eastern Europeans. There were a few Chinese, no Hispanics and no Blacks. We all hung-out together and went to the same schools. Contrary to today's mindset, we really never thought of the fact there were "differences" among our backgrounds. None of us were involved in ethnic activities. We were too young for wakes and weddings, and the only family gatherings were holiday dinners, first communions and confirmation parties.

Whether owing to my youthful naivete or outright stupidity, I have no recollection of any religious or ethnic prejudices or hatred in those days, at least not in my little world, nor among my various playmates. For example, when we spoke of Polack Alley or Jew-Town, we did so simply to identify an area or a neighborhood, not attributing anything derogatory to the appellative. While I don't deny that, among adults, there may have been ethnic and cultural animosities, we young ones had not yet been painted with those brushes.

We did stereotype people then, as we continue to do today, but I completely reject the premise of those who equate stereotyping with prejudice. For example, as a result of Middle Village having so much cemetery acreage, we also had many stone cutters in the gravestone and mausoleum business. Every one of these businesses along Metropolitan Avenue was owned and operated by an Italian. While we may have been guilty of faulty syllogizing, were we really prejudiced for believing that all Italians were stone masons?

We believed all Germans to be dispassionate, workaholics. That's because we never saw them outside the home other than the men coming and going to work and the women hanging wash or sweeping the stoop and sidewalk.

As we got older and discovered the beer gardens over by Fresh Pond Road and the German clubs in Ridgewood, we found out that Germans drank and partied just like everyone else. About that same time, we also discovered the Irish pubs in Rockaway. Up until then, our perception of the Irish was that they were all cops and firemen who worked crazy hours. We didn't know they drank either until we started to frequent the Leitrim House, McGuires, O'Dea's and a few other watering holes at the beach.

The point is, no one was really interested in what you were or weren't.

VIRGINIA MONTERO SEPLOWIN

Perverse fate decreed that I be captivated by dancing—Latin dancing. During the year-long school rehearsals when I saw my peers dance with their visiting boyfriends, the extent of my own unworldliness shocked me. Obviously, while I had been busy studying, going to church, and memorizing the catechism, my school chums were experimenting with more sophisticated activities. I vowed to remedy the lack.

Sooner than I realized, I discovered that dancing for me was not just a pastime. Dancing evoked soul joy. My bones and sinews, heart, and mind responded powerfully to the drum beat and the complex Latin rhythms. Dancing a mambo or a bolero, I sensed a timeless connection with something beyond the present moment. My roots felt anchored in some unconscious dimension when I lost myself in the pulsing sound. Latin dancing was a spiritual ritual; it integrated me; it made me whole.

There was something else that I discovered: In my brief experience, boys who were excellent dancers were generally not interested in pursuing an education. Their aspirations were working-class aspirations—the factory, the restaurant, the hotel job. Like my mother, I wanted more. On the other hand, when I met "American" boys—meaning non-Puerto Rican—I generally found them intellectually stimulating but they had no feel for Latin ways or, better still, for Latin dancing. The warm intimacy of the Hispanic family and Hispanic culture appeared alien to them. As I grew older, it became evident that the toll for crossing cultures was steep.

*

My mother would see to it that I visited my godparents periodically. When I was old enough to visit alone, I always approached the Erasmo La Salle Barbershop with mixed feelings. My ancient, asthmatic godmother, Dona Juana, was warmly affectionate. "God bless you, child," she would say, my visit causing her a paroxym of coughing. "How big you are getting. You'll be a young lady very soon." Always the same words. Then she would place delicious home-made fruit sweets on the table. She knew I loved them.

My godfather, on the other hand, was impersonal. Other than the greeting and the goodbye, he had little to say to me. In place of communication, he would put a thin dime in the palm of my hand. "There, for candy." Then to no one in particular, "I know how much children like candy."

Many years later, I learned that La Salle's Barbershop was an institution. At one time, it had a peppermint-striped column in front of it—probably one of the last in the city. I was to discover that from 1910 on, barbershops were cultural centers for the Puerto Rican community. Erasmo La Salle's Barbershop was one of the first. In addition, he was a fine singer and was the first to cut a record in the United States with a group of Puerto Rican musicians. Of course, at the age of eleven I was ignorant of these facts. All I knew was my mother's opinion, that his barbershop was a den of womanizing, shameless, good-for-nothings.

MOHAMAD BAZZI

As a nine-year-old who had just left his war-torn homeland, I was very confused and insecure. Almost the instant I stepped off the plane at JFK airport I was faced with a critical decision: whether or not to assimilate—bury my past and dive headlong into the melting pot. Assimilating was, by far, the easiest thing to do since I've heard next to nothing about Lebanon or any other Arab country during my six years of schooling in New York. The second, more difficult option was to hold on to my heritage, to remain an Arab in a prejudiced society. I decided to follow the harder course. In so doing, I've had to deal with countless stereotypes depicting all Arabs as terrorists and airplane hijackers. I've had to cope with classmates and teachers who know nothing about the Middle East, let alone my country, and thus cannot appreciate my perspective.

Worst of all, I've had to battle a society in which people constantly urge me to forget all about my past and embrace their vision of the future.

MARIO M. CUOMO

My mother and father are Neopolitan. Actually, they're from just outside Naples, in the Provincia di Salerno. They came to America, with hundreds of thousands of other Italians, in the late twenties, illiterate, without money or property and with only a few friends. My father worked awhile in New Jersey, cleaning what were euphemistically called trenches: they were in fact sewers. He was like most of the other immigrants: powerless but prideful; anguished by a lack of education but ambitious; frightened by a society he didn't know but forceful about making his way in. And always, cursed with that unrelenting Italian passion, the passion for the family; a driving desire to sacrifice a large part of his own life only to make something better for his children; that ultimate humility that gives up nearly everything to the next generation.

By the time he and my mother had their third child, it was clear to him that he would have to do something more than dig "trenches" to provide what he wanted for his family. He opened a grocery store with the few pennies they had saved. It was in South Jamaica, in Queens—an Italian-Black-German-Irish-Polish neighborhood, inhabited by the poor and the nearly poor who lived in close to miserable conditions but were free from real frustration, because they had never experienced much better.

The store was open twenty-four hours a day, and by the time I was born in 1932, during the Depression, my father was making a living from sandwiches he made in the early morning for the construction crews and quick midnight snacks he prepared for the night shift in the factory across the street. In between, his store was the neighborhood corner grocery.

Almost everything he did, he did for his children. The small bankbooks—each small deposit a new dream for his kids. Every dollar a little bit closer to a sit-down reception for my sister Marie's wedding. A little bit better for his children than he and my mother had for themselves. And of the little that was left, he and Momma sent money religiously to the parents they had left behind in Italy.

My father never had a man-to-man talk with me or my brother. My father never had time for long drives in the country, where he could teach us about life. He never had time to counsel us on school; he only had time to insist that we study and get A's and be good.

He never sermonized or lectured. But he taught us, and my mother taught us, every single day—just by being what they were. They taught us the simple values: respect for your family, respect for your obligation to your children and to the parents who made you and raised you.

They taught us all we needed to know about the importance of family to society, and they did this just by being what they were.

SILVIO MARTINEZ PALAU

The action takes place at a restaurant in Queens. At curtain-rise Mr. Martinezz, the owner, comes out of the kitchen door accompanied by Henry, the waiter and Jorg, the cook. One will see a salon (walls painted grey, track—state of the art—lights, neon signs: everything in the room should have an air of gentrification, a trendy, late nineteen-eighties, banal look) with six restaurant tables and a bar in the back.

... Most of the actors will speak with thick Spanish accents and with the infantile rhythm of an English class for the foreign born. The two Americans, Johnny García and the food critic will have native accents.

[from Scene 3, First Act]

MRS. PETERS: *(to Henry, coldly)* What's the special of the day?

HENRY: *(effusively)* Oh, the specialty of today, yes; we have chicken sanocho with fried plátanos and palmito salad. Very good, very good!

MRS. PETERS: Whaat?

MR. PETERS: *(smiling condescendingly and talking to his wife)* It is a soup made of green bananas and chicken. *(imitating Henry's accent)* Very good, very good.

MRS. PETERS: *(still cold, sort of to no one and to both men near)* I want a hamburger, something I can pronounce.

MR. PETERS: I know, woman, but they have very good food here *(winking at Henry)*, right?

HENRY: Yes, Mr. Peters, anything you say, our food is good food, we are here to serve you.

MRS. PETERS: *(despondent)* OK, ok: bring me anything you want. What am I going to do?

 MR. MARTINEZZ: *(who has been nearby, listening to the conversation, to himself, perhaps facing the auditorium, solemn)* Shall we serve hamburgers at English Only Restaurant? Shall we all love french fries and hot dogs, too? Why, yes! Who would eat Latin food in times to come? No one should dare, no one would bear the shame of not feeding/American delicacies. To cook or not to cook/chicken sanocho. To eat or not to eat/more chorizos. That's no dilemma. Should we drink Pepsi-Cola? —Michael Jackson, though he's black, don't matter: I think is good idea. My customers, Hispanic approval, I don't doubt. Shall I serve hamburgers at the English Only Restaurant? Sure! *(going to Mrs. Peters, back to his own self)* Mrs. Peters I am very sorry that we don't have hamburgers, but I guarantee you that beginning tomorrow, we will have everything you want: hamburgers, french fries, Pepsi, chewing gum for bad breath, everything...You have given me a great idea. From now on, everybody has to learn to eat hamburgers, that is the American way.

MRS. PETERS: Yes, indeed.

MR. PETERS: You mean, no more Latin food, Lopez?

MR. MARTINEZZ: Oh, no, Mr. Peters! We'll have tostones . . .

MRS. PETERS: *(interrupting)* What!?

MR. MARTINEZZ: . . . and sanocho for people like you. What I mean is that the Hispanic clientele has to be educated into eating American food. It seem to me that learning to eat hamburgers increase tenfold the possibilities of success for the Hispanic community; and all thank you to your wife *(bowing solemnly to Mrs. Peters)* who gave me the idea. Thank you so much, Mrs. Peters.

MRS. PETERS: Hummm.

Once the Peters are served, they will not stop eating for one second, nor screaming: 'More chicken sanocho'

[Scene 2, Second Act]

Enters Johnny García. He is the stereotype of the Hispanic pimp: white suit, jeweled hands, mustache, fedora hat. He is dripping water from the rain. He stands at the threshold then dashes to a stool at the bar.

HENRY: *(when he finally catches up with him, sighing)* Good afternoon, gentleman, welcome to English Only.

JOHNNY: *(turning to look at Henry, amused at Henry's thick accent and solemn demeanor)* Tráete un café. ¿Tienes Ron Cana? dame uno también. *(while Henry goes away with the order, after saying 'excuse me', Johnny goes to the public phone to make a call)* Yo', it's me. How things? . . . Coño! I told you: that guy don't know what he's doing. Pero, mira: that's the best thing that could've happened. Lo mejor. ¿Qué dijo María? Ha, ha, ha! Oye, ya voy pa'llá en un momento. Oh, and tell that guy not to forget it's Thursday at six. I don't wanna hear of any mixed ups again . . . I'll be there later. *(he hangs up)*

MR. MARTINEZZ: *(advised by Henry of Johnny's Spanish-speaking. When Johnny has sat back at the bar)* Good afternoon, sir. Let me introduce myself: my name is Tony Martinezz and this is my restaurant, English Only. Let me first congratulate you on your impeccable American accent; it is delicious to hear Hispanics talking English so well. But, tell me if I'm wrong: it is my impression that I have not the pleasure of looking at you here in my respectful restaurant before . . .

JOHNNY GARCIA: Say what? Look, jerk: I am trying to have a moment with myself! What are you talking about, American accent? I already order something, don't bug me now. *(looking straight at Martinezz's startled face)* Just beat it, hah? *(Mr. Martinezz beats it and Johnny quietly begins nursing the coffee Henry has just brought)* I don't believe it! What's that sucker talking about, American accent! *(he hisses)*

INTERVIEWS WITH NEIGHBORS, by Joseph Barbato
He is a cab driver, 44, from Singapore, living in Elmhurst:
   In a country where the majority is white, you're spotted right away. You try to get a job in a small town in Wisconsin. Forget about it. They figure you're from Mars. In New York, and especially Queens, there is no such thing. They accept people from everywhere. They used to be the same way. First, there were the English. Then the Germans. Then, the Irish, the Jews and Italians, and the Spanish. Now [laughs] us Orientals are taking over.

She is a mid-fortiesh Chinese and works as a manager in a Manhattan advertising agency. She emigrated as a young child, grew up on the Lower East Side ("I thought the Puerto Ricans were the Americans"), and lives in Elmhurst:

Many of the Koreans coming in now are very arrogant. When I first heard about that dispute in Brooklyn involving the black customer in the Korean store, I didn't believe it. But then it happened to me, and *I'm* Oriental. I was in a novelty store with my daughter, and the cashier was Korean. And when I see an Oriental face, I feel glad. I feel, oh, another person from my country, or from the same culture. I gave her the money. She had her hand out, and then she pulled it back. So I left the money on the counter, and then she gave me the change. She slapped the money on the counter. Didn't even give me a thank-you. I didn't quite understand it, but I felt very ashamed to be Oriental. Yet some Koreans are very polite and friendly.

Discrimination will always be there. It's going to take a long, long time for people to advance and look at each other without saying, oh, you are from here, and I'm from there. You have to get to know the person and feel comfortable.

She is a Korean woman in her thirties. In 1981, she and her husband, a salesman with a furniture company in Flushing, Queens, came here so he could earn a degree. They have two young school-age children. There is a set of the Encyclopedia Britannica *in the living room of their Jackson Heights home:*

I was a teacher in my country. I taught elementary school. Here, I make handbags in a factory. A lot of the people I work with are from Colombia and the Dominican Republic. They never remember anything. Every time they have to do something, even if they've done it a hundred times before, they have to ask how. They don't have any education. I feel badly about how I feel about them.

It was a difficult decision to come here. I was scared, but we wanted a better life. We left my family in Seoul, my parents and my brothers and sisters. My husband's mother and father came with us. They hate it here. They watch the kids while I work. I'd like to be a teacher here, but I have to take more courses, and I can't. I have to help pay the mortgage. On

Saturdays, I teach at the Korean school. I teach Korean to my people.

I wish I could go back to Korea. It would be better there. Here, there are many people from different countries, and some look down on Koreans, especially the Spanish and black people. There are many crimes. Our car was stolen a week after we moved into this house.

But I can't go back to Korea. My friends and family have good jobs. I'd be ashamed to go back to my country. I have to be here. I have to put roots down. I have to get used to it. But sometimes it's hard. Many things happen. Some black people treat us badly. Not all of them; some black people are good. Some Korean people are bad too. But we all have to be friends. We're all one family, God's family. It has nothing to do with where you're from, or what you look like.

At night, my son prays before he goes to bed. He says, "God, give us a chance to make a lot of money."

They live several blocks from a restaurant where the editor of El Diario, *the Spanish-language daily, was slain several weeks earlier. They are natives of Baghdad, Iraq, of Armenian descent. Their marriage was arranged. He is forty-four, an inspector with a state agency; she is much younger, a homemaker taking business courses at night. They have two sons, ages eleven and six, and live in a one-bedroom apartment in Elmhurst. Both speak heavily accented English. He dominates the conversation—these are his words, except where she interrupts:*

The American Dream is gone. It's finished. A family should be able to afford a house, an education for the children, and food. This country is so rich and powerful, it should be able to make American dreams come true again.

I came here at twenty-three. I came because I saw many American movies with Burt Lancaster, and Robert Mitchum, and Spencer Tracy. The United States seemed different, and I wanted to be an actor. I landed at JFK airport, went to the Armenian church on 27th Street in Manhattan, and met some people there. Where do you want to go? they asked me. California? Stay in New York? One man had a shoe factory in Massachusetts and was going back that night. I went with him to Worcester. Later, I came here.

American movies gave me a sense of a different culture and free way of life. They showed me you could get ahead. And I was very ambitious. I had two years of college in my country, and I wanted to get somewhere. But it didn't come true. My disappointments were many. I left my family—eight brothers and a sister, my mother and father, and my grandmother. There, families are united and you see them every day. I was close to them. I loved them.

But I was very young, and I came here, and I saw what loneliness means. You try to achieve something, and it takes a long time. Then you start to think, what did you gain? What did you lose? I lost a lot. One of my brothers died, at thirty, and I wasn't there. My father died, and I wasn't there. I was here alone, working. And when I had trouble, there was no one to help or give advice.

There's a lack of acceptance. Americans don't trust foreigners. I don't know where it comes from. They simply don't trust, no matter what you do. I didn't believe there was discrimination in this country. I was young. When I matured, I saw more clearly. And I can't blame people who don't like foreigners. It's their country. Yes, you were born here. Your father and your grandfather were born here. Why do you want me here? You don't want me. I accept that.

I have people telling me, go back to your country. Pure Americans, who were born here and have no accent. They will tell you, go back where you came from. But I pay my taxes. Maybe I love this country more than they love it. I can't go back to my country. I have been in this country for so many years, I have been away from so many things. Maybe my country doesn't want me anymore. I am an American citizen now.

*

Wife: Iraq wasn't our country either. We were born there,

but we are Armenians.

*

Where we come from, people were close. They were more religious. Materialistic things change people. When our people came here, and saw they could afford houses or cars, they started straying from each other. They come here, and they change. The closeness is gone. It's not like in the Middle East. The more you have here, the more you withdraw from others. This happens in families, even between mothers and daughters. I cannot blame them. I did not succeed in life very much. Maybe that's why they withdraw. Is that success? Progress? If I knew how much I was going to lose, what I would go through, I would have stayed in Iraq and been more successful. I know the way of life, I know the way things are.

*

Wife: Over there, people come to your home. They go to parties. They laugh. Here, you go to work, come home, and there is nothing to do if you don't have money. You make more money here, but life is more expensive.

*

As for the other people here, I have many Indian and Korean friends at work. Most are into their own communities. They prefer to be with their own people. They go to their own churches and clubs. It's different for the kids. They make friends at school and play together. I would like to have good friends from other cultures, but if I don't, I don't worry about it.

*

Wife: I'm friendlier than him. I don't think badly about any person. For me, people are all the same. I talk at business school, and I give people my phone number. I tell them, come for coffee. They think I'm not serious. They don't come.

*

There is fear. You get comfortable with your own culture. You don't know what other people like. Sometimes, there's a language barrier. You sit with them, but what language are you going to speak? Maybe they don't speak English.

If our kids are going to live here, they have to Americanize. That's why I put American names on them. So many people who were born here still have accents. People think they're foreigners. For our kids, this is their country. They were born here. They have to Americanize completely. She doesn't agree. She would like to see them in Armenian school [the children attend the local public school].

*

Wife: We are Armenians first. I want them to know more about our culture. I want them to learn Armenian.

*

It would be better for them to learn French or Japanese. They could use it in business.

*

Wife: Now that Armenia is free, maybe they could be ambassadors to there. We Armenians are a proud people. We are survivors. Wherever you put us, we get ahead. When my sons go to the Armenian church and hold a candle, they feel *proud*. I like to see them *proud* of something.

*

As long as they don't have accents in English. I want them to learn fluent, accentless English.

SUSAN ORLEAN

The *Times* had run a story saying that Roosevelt Avenue had become the city's largest prostitution center outside Manhattan, and that brothels staffed with South American and Asian girls were operating all along it.

In the mid-eighties, police noted that thousands of Chinese immigrants, many of them illegal, were moving into neighborhoods in Queens, including Jackson Heights, and were establishing criminal organizations, known as tongs, whose roots could be traced back to the eighteen-fifties. Around the same time, members of the Shining Path, the Peruvian Maoist terrorist group, were rumored to have established their North American headquarters in Jackson Heights. Also in the eighties, it became widely known that Jackson Heights was one of the most important centers for Colombian cocaine traffic in this country .... And in March, 1992, a journalist named Manuel de Dios Unanue, the Cuban-born former editor of *El Diario-La Prensa*, who often reported on drug cartels, many of them operating out of Jackson Heights, and on political corruption, was shot twice in the back of the head and killed while eating dinner at Mesón Asturias, one of a dozen Argentine restaurants in the neighborhood.

Jackson Heights used to be a region of productive farms, part of an area known as Newtown. In 1909, Edward A. Mac-Dougall, a real-estate developer, began buying land in the area, and later renamed it in honor of John Jackson .... The apartment houses MacDougall developed were innovative. Many were built European style, with a square block of apartments enclosing a garden courtyard. And many of the buildings had automatic elevators, which meant that they could be six stories high, instead of the five then standard in Queens. Also, MacDougall offered the apartments for collective ownership; they were among the first co-op apartments in America.... By and large the neighborhood consisted of middle-class Italians, Irish, and Jews until 1965, when immigration quotas were loosened and thousands of South and Central Americans, Koreans, Indians, Chinese, and Southeast Asians came to the United States. Jackson Heights, which was generally quieter, cleaner, safer, and prettier than similarly inexpensive neighborhoods in Manhattan, Brooklyn, or the Bronx, held great appeal.

Jackson Heights now has a hundred and twenty-nine thousand residents. Twenty-eight percent are white; forty-three percent are Hispanic; fifteen and a half percent are black; eleven and a half percent are Asian. More than half of the ninety-four thousand Indians in New York City live in Queens—mainly in Jackson Heights and Flushing. Soviet immigrants are forming a settlement in the neighborhood. There is a chain of Uruguayan bakeries on Thirty-seventh Avenue. Jackson Heights is the de-facto capital of the Argentine community in the United States. In some ways, the various nationalities have blended together, but in other ways, even in this small, crowded space, they have managed to remain clearly articulated. A sari shop and a Dominican diner side by side on the same block can still manage to feel ten thousand miles apart.

DEPARTMENT OF CITY PLANNING

Elmhurst is perhaps the most ethnically mixed community in the world, with 17,200 new immigrants from 118 countries who arrived between 1983 and 1989 alone.... Queens, particularly Elmhurst, Flushing and Astoria, played host to the greatest number and most diverse population of new immigrants. More than 36 percent of the borough is now foreign-born. The Chinese dominated the new immigrant wave to Queens, followed by the Guyanese, the Dominicans and the Colombians.

ROGER SANJEK

It is my guess, and here there is much need for historical research, that "white" people have become much more self-conscious of an inclusive racial identity in the past twenty-five years than they were throughout most of Queens history. The numbers of black, Chinese, and Hispanic Queens residents have been tiny until these recent years. In the majority's eyes, "Queens was white," to paraphrase [Jimmy] Breslin. But "white" was not the principal operant social identity. Rather it was Dutch, English, German, Irish, Italian, Polish, Jewish, Greek, or another European nationality, or, for some, simply "American."...

The First Presbyterian Church of Newtown today includes in its congregation a mix of Scottish, German, Irish, Swedish, Czech and other white American members. The oldest church in Elmhurst, dating to 1652, First Presbyterian over the years has seen the meeting and accommodation of diverse European groups. But today, it is also an international church, with Filipino, Indian, Indonesian, Chinese, Puerto Rican, Mexican, Cuban, Trinidadian, St. Vincentian, Barbadian, Ghanaian, Kenyan and Black American members. It is a united, integrated congregation, with one English-language service, and one schedule of social activities, attended by all. . . .

It is true that racial differences are more striking in Queens now than Queens then. But, as we have noted, ethnic differences among Europeans have seen their disjunctive and disruptive periods. Bonds among those Europeans who became white Americans formed slowly, but form they did. Queens now provides us with interesting questions to ask of the historical record. In turn, the past may offer us lessons about what to expect amidst the ongoing complexities of Queens today, and tomorrow.

CHEN HSIANG-SHUI

T The first Chinese to live and work in Queens were probably laundry workers and truck farmers. Hand laundries opened in middle-class and working-class residential areas where families had enough money to send out white shirts and collars, but not enough money to hire washerwomen to work in their homes. The older communities of Astoria, Long Island City, Newtown and Flushing no doubt had hand laundries from the 1880s onward. These laundries were usually operated by two partners. They worked twelve-, sixteen-, twenty-hour days, six days a week. These worker/owners would live in the back of the laundries both to save money and to avoid difficulties in renting quarters in non-Chinese neighborhoods. Laundry workers in New York called this life an "eight-pound livelihood," referring to the weight of the iron they would be carrying around all day. Others called it a "blood-and-tears" existence. . . .

Shen Ho Joe is credited by *The New York Times* as being the first Chinese farmer in Queens during the 1880s. Realizing that fresh Chinese vegetables would be of great value to the residents and restaurants of Chinatown, he rented several acres of land from an Astoria florist. Transportation costs across the East River were minimal, especially in comparison to vegetables shipped from Chinese farms in California. He borrowed start-up money. For $600 a year in rent, he built a successful business. Soon five other Chinese truck farms opened in Astoria, and an additional two started in Steinway and Flatbush. Innovative fertilizing techniques yielded four crops a year. Bitter melon (*kugua*, which sold for sixty-five cents a pound), *bok choy*, white turnips (*luopo*), hairy squash (*maogua*), Chinese broccoli (*jielan*), and many other items were grown with good results. Some of the farms operated until 1922 when the Astoria Gardens housing complex was built on their rented land. Some tantalizing evidence of Chinese and Euro-American interaction is offered by one newspaper account of that era. Local white boys were said to have "often increased their spending allowances by helping 'John Chinaman' cultivate his farm."

The size of the Queens Chinese population was tiny at the turn of the century, no more than 150 in all. Up to 1920, the New York City census category "other" (those neither white nor black) consisted mainly of Chinese, along with a few Japanese. In 1900, there were 153 "others" in Queens; 152 in 1910; and 261 in 1920.

RODLYN H. DOUGLAS

As it is for you as a Black American, it is for me as a Black West Indian. I am faced with the same prejudices, same resentments, same being passed over for someone who is white even though they may not have my ability, knowledge and education. . . .

When white America looks out all they see is Black, period.

Prejudice sees and knows no difference between West Indian Black and American Black.

There was a time when white America tried to pit us one against the other, forcing a wedge of hate and resentment between us by comparing our working habits and social attitudes, our ability to struggle and survive despite the shackles. They would look at me and smile cunningly, "oh, you are not Black, you are West Indian . . . I just love that accent and that smile . . ." But that time is long past. Now, united in the struggle we must forget our geographic differences and concentrate on learning what we can from each other as sisters and brothers of Mother Africa, people of color determined to overcome the obstacles and barriers of divide-and-conquer placed in our paths by the white Americans who would have us believe that this land is God's gift to them. This land of the free and home of the brave. Yes, you are free, Black America, and brave. Take up your bravery as you did your freedom and work towards your life's goals. Look at me! Unless I open my mouth and speak, you would never know there is a difference between us. Now, is there really? Or is it a perceived difference that exists only in your fear of being overlooked? I am your brother, I am your sister, we are in this struggle together. Yes, my accent is funny and I may like dressing in bright tropical colors—I am West Indian—that doesn't mean I am not Black.

Ed DuRanté
HOMEBOYS

Scene 4

A few days later in the park, about 6 p.m., Troy walks up to the usual hang-out spot. He has a bottle of diet Coke in one hand and his ghetto blaster on his shoulder. A reggae tune is playing. He puts the box down and takes a long swig. Suddenly the reggae song ends and Elvis' "Blue Suede Shoes" begins. This is Troy's favorite Elvis tune. He begins gyrating his hips and dancing Elvis-style. While Troy is caught up in the music, Ed walks up wearing a McDonald's uniform and carrying a basketball. He is visible to the audience, but Troy doesn't notice him. Ed watches for a while and then laughs hysterically.

ED: What are you doing, practicing for Soul Train?

TROY: (*startled, he turns off the tape*) Oh, excuse me. I was briefly possessed by the spirit of the King. So . . . what's up?

ED: Nothing much. I just got off work. I caught one of those new buses and let me tell you, that ride was sweet. It had air conditioning, clean seats and you know the part of Hollis that looks like main street Beirut?

Troy takes Ed's ball and tries to do some fancy dribbling. He fails terribly.

TROY: Unh huh.

ED: Well, I didn't feel one pothole. I mean, smooth as Whitney Houston's behind. Hey, can I have some of that?

TROY: (*he hands Ed the bottle*) Just don't kill it.

Ed turns up the bottle as if to finish it. Troy tries to grab it but Ed pushes him away.

TROY: Come on man, don't be a pig.

Ed belches loudly and then hands the bottle to Troy.

ED: (*he takes a deep breath*) Let me tell you, burning burgers is not as easy as I thought. (*He looks at his arms and rubs them.*) I got grease burns all over my arms and I smell like a Big Mac.

TROY: (*fanning the air*) You should wish you smelled like a Big Mac.

ED: (*he sniffs himself*) Thank god it's only for a couple of months. I'd go crazy if I had to do this for a living.

TROY: Don't you want to go to Hamburger U. and get a degree in professional grillmanship? Why not be all that you can be. Remember, it's more than a job, it's an adventure. McDonald's is looking for a few ...

Ed grabs Troy and puts his hand over his mouth.

ED: You been looking at too much tv. Why don't you get a summer job?

TROY: I know misery loves company, but I think I'll pass. I'm too busy to get a job anyway.

ED: Too busy? Busy doing what?

TROY: Well, actually, I'm involved with a few projects, the foremost being an all-out effort to watch every episode of the Andy Griffith Show, and the secondary ...

ED: Hold it! You're ... you're gonna try and watch every ...

TROY: Well, of course I don't expect to see them all this summer. It's my long-term project.

ED: So what's the short-term project?

TROY: I've begun work on a novel.

ED: That's short-term.

TROY: So it's a novella, anyway, it's entitled *Urban Rites*.

ED: What the hell do you mean by Urban Rights? I've heard of civil rights, women's rights, children's rights, even animal rights, but urban rights?

TROY: Ed, you're talking about the wrong rites!

ED: Then shouldn't it be Urban Writings?

TROY: No, No! I mean rites as in rituals, as in rites of passage!

ED: Well, why didn't you say so? (*Ed dribbles the ball.*) What's it about?

TROY: That's a complex matter. It's about life, it's about love, it's about survival in the city. Of course it won't be seminal, but ...

ED: Seminal?

TROY: Seminal.

ED: Is this going to be some kinda sex book? I mean, I know you've been reading all those sex manuals and stuff, but you don't know enough to write a book.

TROY: It's not a sex book, okay!

ED: Okay.

TROY: Anyway, the reason I brought this up is I want your opinion about one of the characters. You see, he's going to be based upon a mutual friend of ours.

ED: Oh yeah, who?

TROY: First you have to swear to me that this conversation stays between you and me.

ED: Okay.

TROY: Seriously man, I need you to swear.

ED: Okay, okay, I swear. Mum's the word, alright. My word is my bond.

TROY: The reason I'm talking to you about this is because I don't believe you will be all that surprised about what I'm a-bout to suggest. I say that because you have said some things that made me think that you have come to some of the same conclusions that I have.

ED: Get to the point.

TROY: It's about Andre Wheeler, also known as Snake, the self-proclaimed dog extraordinaire and subliminal seducer.

ED: You're going to base one of your characters on Snake? It *is* a sex book!

TROY: I'm serious, man!

ED: I'm sorry. Okay, what do you want to know?

TROY: Actually, I don't really want to ask a question. I'm going to make a statement and I want you to respond immediately, a gut reaction. No thinking.

ED: Bet.

TROY: Okay, are you ready?

ED: Go ahead!

TROY: I think . . . well, it seems possible that . . . uh . . . uh . . .

ED: Say it!

TROY: I think Snake's a homosexual.

Ed does not react or say a word.

TROY: Well?

ED: Well, what?

TROY: I was right. You think he is too.

ED: I didn't say that.

TROY: So what do you think?

ED: I think it's possible.

TROY: (*nervously*) I think it's probable. Now don't get me wrong. I'm not judging him if he's gay. I just think it's a bit bizarre . . . no, intriguing . . . you know what I mean, considering his personality. But on second thought, I guess it all kind of fits together. All that macho stuff is merely a facade; an attempt to repress his natural proclivities. (*pause*) Do you think he has ever actually . . .

ED: (*calmly*) Fucked a guy? Nah. I don't think so. I think he may have thought about it, but I think he's totally in the closet.

TROY: Yeah, you're probably right. He probably doesn't really know it himself. He'll probably never do it. Right? He has occasional homosexual thoughts, but he'll never actually approach another . . . another man. Would he?

Long pause. They stare at one another and then speak simultaneously.

ED & TROY: Nah!

TROY: Of course not. Hey, it's just a phase.

ED: Yeah, a phase. (*a beat*) Hey.

TROY: A phase, definitely a phase.

ED: I think he's in love with Killer.

TROY: Me too.

ED: You're in love with Killer, too? (*They both laugh.*) This is some wild shit man.

TROY: Yeah, and it's going to make my book a best seller.

ED: You think Killer knows?

TROY: Now be serious. Of course he doesn't know! He's a stereotypical homophobe. If he thought Snake was gay it would be all over.

ED: You know, all of this explains why Snake hates Eve.

TROY: This explains a lot of things.

ED: We joked around about it, but he's actually jealous of her.

TROY: Neither one of us was joking and you know it. We both thought this for a while now and we both, well at least I, was going for a reaction. Everytime I jokingly questioned his masculinity or insinuated he was gay I was looking for a reaction.

ED: You're pretty sneaky for a Rasta.

TROY: Don't start!

ED: I'm not starting anything. I'm just surprised that you picked up on this.

TROY: I'm surprised you haven't called him out on it. I mean, you don't exactly have a record of being incredibly tolerant of alternative lifestyles.

ED: What did you expect me to do—run around the neighborhood yelling, "Snake's a faggot, Snake's a faggot!"

TROY: I don't know what I expected, but the other night when I drank you under the proverbial table, you almost let the proverbial cat out of the proverbial closet.

ED: Did I?

TROY: Did you? You called him a faggot and then went into your "walk like a duck, talk like a duck" routine.

ED: Shit!

TROY: Shit? Shit? Is that all you can say?

ED: You don't think he knows we know?

TROY: I doubt it.

ED: What should we do?

TROY: What can we do? Are you going to be the one to tell Killer that his homeboy is a ho...

Andre arrives as Troy is about to say homosexual. To cover, Troy swings his bottle and sings.

TROY: Ho, ho, the pirate's life for me.

ANDRE: Que pasa amigos?

ED: Just hangin' man. What's up with you?

ANDRE: (*pointing to the bottle*) Not much. Hey can I kill that?

TROY: Not unless you're gonna buy me another bottle.

ANDRE: (*handing Ed money*) Okay, Ed, why don't you get another bottle of Diet Coke and a couple Olde E for us.

ED: Alright!

Ed exits.

TROY: My, you're being unusually generous today.

ANDRE: What can I say, I'm in a good mood.

TROY: (*suspicious*) What's with you? Is it potlatch season already?

ANDRE: Huh?

TROY: Sorry, just a bad joke. What's with this sudden surge of generosity?

ANDRE: I told you, I'm in a good mood.

TROY: Give me a break.

ANDRE: Really. For the last couple of weeks I've been real tense. I've been thinking about my future. About our future.

TROY: Referring to whom?

ANDRE: Referring to you, me, Ed, and Killer.

TROY: What about our future?

ANDRE: We've been hanging together for as long as I can remember and . . . and . . . uh . . . you guys are the only real friends I've got. And . . . uh . . . uh . . . I'm just starting to worry that we're drifting apart. Shit, we usta do everything together.

TROY: I don't believe this. You actually care? I always got the impression that you didn't give a damn whether you saw us or not.

ANDRE: Well, you know . . . you see, I got an image to keep up.

TROY: Ahh, yes. I forgot.

ANDRE: But really, with you and Ed off at college, things are gonna be boring as hell around here.

TROY: Your boy will still be here.

ANDRE: Shit, Killer's been spending so much time with that bitch, I hardly ever see him.

TROY: Why do you talk about Eve like that? He really loves her.

ANDRE: I don't give a fuck. Me and Killer usta be like this (*he shows crossed fingers*) until he started seeing that ... that ... shit, she's not even that good looking. What's he see in her? We all like a steady piece, but she can't be that good in bed. I mean, a piece'a ass is a piece'a ass.

TROY: You've got the wrong idea about them. Like I said, he really loves her. And believe it or not, they have yet to make the beast with two backs.

ANDRE: What the fuck are you talking about?

TROY: I was talking to William a couple of days ago and we were discussing women, as usual, and one thing lead to another and we started talking about him and Eve. And, well apparently, they have never had sexual intercourse.

ANDRE: (*shocked*) What?

TROY: Really, he said that she was a virgin and she refuses to relinquish her maidenhead until she is married. He admitted he was quite frustrated at first, but he claims that he loves her so much that he's willing to put up with it. He's a better man than I.

ANDRE: (*incredulous*) I don't believe it! I just can't believe that Killer hasn't . . . he's Killer. It doesn't make any sense.

TROY: To be honest, I don't think he has pushed the issue. I don't know why, but I got the distinct impression that he's almost glad that he hasn't . . . you know, deflowered her.

ANDRE: Come on.

TROY: He seemed almost relieved that for once he didn't have to live up to his reputation. You know what I mean? (*pause*) It seems he's tired of being The Killer. He even said he has given up all his other ladies.

ANDRE: Are you telling me that he's not even screwing other women?

TROY: You got it.

Ed returns with two bottles of Olde E and a Diet Coke. They all get a bottle and start drinking.

ED: Wait a minute. Let's make a toast.

They raise their bottles to toast.

ED: To the good ole days and the good ole days to come.

They drink and raise bottles again.

ANDRE: To all the girls I used to love and to those who haven't been so lucky.

They laugh and drink. Troy starts his toast, but Ed and Andre continue drinking, laughing, and ad-lib bullshittin'.

TROY: To ... (*pause*) ... to be or not to be, that is the question. Whether 'tis nobler in the mind to suffer the slings and arrows of outrageous fortune or to take arms against a sea of trouble and by opposing, end them. To die, to sleep, no more. And by a sleep to say we ... we ... end ... end ... we end the heartache, and the thousand natural shocks that flesh is heir to!

In the middle of Troy's Hamlet rendition William runs on the scene. He is out of breath. Ed and Andre greet him while Troy continues his toast.

WILLIAM: What's up?

Ed spins his ball on his finger.

ED: Yo!

ANDRE: What's up?

WILLIAM: (*slowly*) Fellas, I got some surprising news.

ANDRE: Oh yeah, what's that?

William speaks the moment Troy finishes with "... heir to!"

WILLIAM: I'm getting married.

Ed sprays out a mouth full of Olde E. There is a long silence. They look back and forth at one another. Andre stands motionless, staring at William.

ED: You're lying!

WILLIAM: No bullshit. I'm getting married and the sooner the better.

ED: Man, you didn't . . . I mean . . . Eve's not pregnant is she?

WILLIAM: Nope.

ED: What the hell you getting married for if you didn't knock her up?

TROY: What kind of thing is that to say? Let me be the first to congratulate you. (*Troy shakes William's hand.*) But I have one question: why now?

WILLIAM: Because I just got notice that I passed the police test and I start the police academy in September.

TROY: Excuse my ignorance, but I didn't know that marriage was a prerequisite for employment with New York's finest.

WILLIAM: I told Eve that I would marry her as soon as I got a good-paying job. Now I got it and I'm gonna marry her.

ED: A cop. You're going to be an officer of the law. That's more of a shock than the marriage. You've been seeing Eve—what, about a year now?

William nods.

TROY: Well, I guess it's about time you made an honest woman out of her. But you, a cop—man, that's a trip. And I suppose Andre here will be your first arrest.

Troy laughs, but then realizes the serious implications of all this. There is a brief silence.

TROY: Well . . . uh . . . have you set a date for the nuptials?

WILLIAM: Not yet, but soon. Real soon. Pop's so happy that

I passed the test that he said he'll get rid of the bar so me and Eve can move into the basement. Just until I can afford a place of my own, of course.

ED: Well, let me be the second to congratulate you.

Ed and William hug. Ed hands him a bottle. William takes a long drink.

WILLIAM: So . . . Snake, you willing to be my best man or what?

Andre closes his eyes and shakes his head and then responds with feigned enthusiasm.

ANDRE: You know it, homeboy!

Andre and William hug. Everybody drinks. Troy turns on his boom box. The remainder of "Blue Suede Shoes" plays.

ED: Time to celebrate!

TROY: Blue Ice, here we come!

Ed, Troy, and William move to exit.

ANDRE: I'll meet you guys over there. I got some shit I got to do first.

WILLIAM: Hurry up, 'cause we're gonna wait outside 'til you get there.

ANDRE: It'll just take a coupla'a minutes. I'll be right there.

WILLIAM: Alright, I'll see you in a few.

William runs off to catch Ed and Troy.

Andre watches his friends leave. He leans up against the fence, pulls out a joint, lights it and smokes. Between drags he drinks. He shakes his head and begins to laugh. The laughter is soft at first but becomes gradually louder.

Suddenly he stops laughing. He throws the bottle. It shatters.

Blackout.

Scene 5

Andre is knocking on Eve's door. He can be seen stage left. He knocks very loudly. A light comes on in the apartment. Eve is lying on a bed that is on the floor center stage. At its head is a bright fluorescent desk lamp, a telephone, and an alarm clock. Upstage and right is a free-standing full-length mirror. Eve turns on the lamp and then looks at the clock. She gets up. She is wearing a sexy night gown. She looks through the peephole and then opens the door.

EVE: Snake, it's four in the morning. What are you doing here?

ANDRE: Visiting.

EVE: I don't want any visitors at four in the morning (*looking out the door and then closing it*) Where's William? I thought he was going out with you guys.

ANDRE: He got plastered and Ed took him home.

EVE: What do you want, anyway?

ANDRE: I want to talk to you.

EVE: Can't it wait?

ANDRE: No! It can't wait.

EVE: What? What do you want?

ANDRE: I want to know why you're doing this to Killer.

EVE: Doing what?

ANDRE: Why are you making him marry you.

EVE: You don't know what you're talking about.

ANDRE: Sure, sure. I know all about your type. You make a man do things he never would have done. Do things he never even thought about. (*a beat*) My man. Why are you taking my man? My homeboy. He don't wanna get married. You just got his nose wide open. How can he be so . . . so goddamn stupid. He thinks you're some kinda goddess. He thinks you're pure as the muthafuckin' driven snow, but you ain't nothin' but a bitch in heat! You're just a good for nothin' whoe!

Eve slaps Andre. He then grabs her arms.

ANDRE: So you wanna play rough. Well, I can play that game too.

Andre pushes Eve onto the bed. He gets on top of her and holds her arms down. He starts kissing her. She struggles to escape.

EVE: No! No! Snake, what are you doing?

ANDRE: You know what I'm doing!

Eve continues to struggle, and screams.

EVE: Don't do this Snake! Please, don't do this!

ANDRE: Don't do this? (*He gets up off of Eve*) The other night you begged me to do this. What's wrong? Is something different now? You're not feeling well? No, I get it. I know what you need. You're always in the mood after a few lines.

Andre takes a bag of coke out of his pocket and throws it at her.

ANDRE: Right, Miss Chastity? Right Miss I'm-saving-myself-for-my-husband?

EVE: (*crying*) Stop it, Snake! Stop it!

ANDRE: Now it's "Stop it, Snake!" You know, you're too fuckin' much. If you think I'm gonna let you marry Killer, you must be out your muthafuckin' mind.

EVE: (*starting to compose herself*) Yeah, you're gonna let me marry him. You know why? (*She stands.*) Because you can't tell your best friend, your homeboy, that you've been screwin' his lady! (*confidentially*) Face it, you've lost him. He's mine! You tell him and he'll hate you for the rest of your life. And you couldn't bear that thought, could you? Could you, tough guy?

Andre sits on the futon and stares at the floor.

ANDRE: Why did he have to fall in love with you? It doesn't make any sense.

EVE: It makes plenty of sense. I planned it. Yeah, I played with his mind. I love him more than anything, but he never would have fallen in love with me if he knew I...I shit! You think I wanna be screwin' niggas like you for the rest of my life? To get Killer to want to marry me I had to be different, so I played the role. I came off like the sweet innocent young thang that every man wants to take home to mama. Is that so wrong? Is it wrong to want to be loved? All I wanted was to be respected and loved, but he never would have respected me if he really knew about me. Why? Because I've been around. Because I screw when I get horny. Shit, you guys go around screwin' everything eight to eighty and it's cool, but if I want a little fun I'm a slut. I'm good enough for you to screw, but I'm not good enough to marry your boy? Fuck you, Snake! Fuck you! Me and Killer are getting married and there's nothing you can do about it!

pause

ANDRE: I can't believe this is happening.

Andre gets up and goes to the full-length mirror. He stares at his reflection. He speaks slowly. It is uncertain whether he is talking to himself or to Eve.

ANDRE: Why didn't you stop me?

EVE: Why the fuck didn't you stop yourself? Shit, I'm not kidding myself. I know I was wrong. I didn't want you. I wanted Killer. But no, he had to make his stupid point. At first I thought it was my fault. I tried everything. But the more I tried the more he hung out with you. I just couldn't take it so I decided to let you get as far as you would go. (*short pause*) You know the rest. (*short pause*) But don't you even think that it was because you were some kinda smooth operator, because everytime we were together I was wishing it was Killer. You were a tool, a walking, talking vibrator! Sure, it was stupid and immoral and believe me I regret it. It was the biggest mistake of my life. But it's over now. Finally, it's over and I'm gonna spend the rest of my life making it up to him.

ANDRE: (*staring at Eve*) I have to tell him.

EVE: (*frantic*) No you don't! What good will it do? It'll ruin everything!

ANDRE: But...

EVE: No one will benefit from his knowing. For once be a man!

Andre sits on the bed in a trance-like state.

ANDRE: Me and Killer met in the third grade.

EVE: He'll hate you!

ANDRE: His moms walked him to the bus stop. Once we got on the bus he just sat there looking out the window. Everyone else was jumping up and down and screaming. He just sat there.

EVE: He'll never forgive you!

ANDRE: He had curly hair and new clothes.

EVE: Please, Snake!

ANDRE: He always raised his hand. Everytime Mrs.... uh... Abrams, Mrs. Abrams asked a question, up went his hand. I hated that. Once I was sitting in the back of the room. I was in trouble for something. Anyway, on that day Mrs. Abrams asked a question and as usual he raised his hand. He was the only one, but she wouldn't call on him. She called on five or six other kids and none of them knew the answer. Then all of a sudden he screamed out "Crispus Attucks, Crispus Attucks!" She was pissed. She sent him to the back with me. We sat there not saying a word to each other. Then he started mumbling. After a while I realized he was cussing Mrs. Abrams. I started laughing and she yelled at me. Then we were both cussing her out. Anyway, she asked the class what was the "shot heard 'round the world." No one knew so she called on me. I didn't know either, but then Killer raised his hand. Then she said, "William, I'm glad you have learned to wait until you're called on. Now what was the shot heard 'round the world?" He stood up, cleared his throat, and cut the loudest fart I ever heard. (*he laughs*) I swear that was the funniest shit I've ever seen. We must have laughed for ten minutes. He got in big trouble, but hey, it was worth it. (*pause*) He was so cool.

The audience sees William run up to Eve's door. He bends over and puts his hands on his knees while he tries to catch his breath.

EVE: Snake, go home and think about it. You'll see I'm right.

William knocks on the door. Eve and Andre look at one another. Eve walks over to the door.

EVE: Who is it?

WILLIAM: (*drunk and out of breath*) It's me baby.

EVE: Killer?

Eve looks through the peephole and then lets him in.

WILLIAM: I'm sorry I'm so late. The fellas took me out to celebrate and as you can see, I had a little too much.

EVE: Didn't Ed take you home?

WILLIAM: Yeah, but, like I said, I had a few more than I should have and I forgot I said I would come over tonight, so I ran over here.

ANDRE: You ran all the way from your house?

WILLIAM: Yep, all the way from 208th and Hollis. You know, if I was sober I never could have done that. Maybe runners should get drunk before races and...Snake?! What are you doing here? Didn't you say...

ANDRE: Yeah, I did...um...I took care'a that and...uh... since I was in the neighborhood, I...ah...figured I'd stop by and tell Eve that you were drunk and that Ed took you home.

WILLIAM: Hey, man, thanks a lot. You see, that's why he's gonna be the best man. He looks out for me. (*He puts his arm around Andre.*) If you never get no bigger, you'll always be my nigga. (*He plops down on the bed.*) Look at this. If we had a priest we could get married now. The bride, the groom, the best man. Let's call the priest.

William sits up, grabs the phone and starts dialing. Eve takes the phone away and hangs it up.

EVE: Come on, Killer, lie down and go to sleep.

William lies down and closes his eyes.

ANDRE: I guess I'll be going now.

William opens his eyes and sits up a little.

WILLIAM: Alright, thanks a lot man. I'll talk to you.

Andre leaves and Eve locks the door behind him. She turns off the light and then lies down next to William.

EVE: Let's go to sleep.

William sits up slowly and begins undressing.

WILLIAM: That Snake is something else.

EVE: Yeah, something else.

fade out

Scene 6

RAPPER: *My word is my bond*
                    Is a common claim
                    The truth will set you free
                    These words inflame
                    Lies told to friends
                    Leave a stench in the room
                    A Judas kiss
                    From best man to groom
                    Fabrication a hobby
                    But many go pro
                    Scouts honor?
                    Bull!
                    Honesty a show
                    Abernathy told a lie
                    Benny Arnold was a spy
                    Et tu Brute
                    I thought you were my friend
                    But push come to shove
                    You were a Judas in the end

The scene opens in the waiting room of the church where William is to marry Eve. All the homeboys wear white tuxedos with tails. Center stage is a door that opens into the room. On it hangs a large crucifix. On both sides of the door are six folding chairs.

Ed paces, dribbling his basketball in front of William, who sits calmly in a chair stage left of the door.

WILLIAM: Why don't you calm down? If I didn't know better I'd think you were the one getting married.

ED: I'm just a little nervous. I've never been in a wedding before.

WILLIAM: Come on, sit down. You're making me nervous.

Ed sits next to William. Ed taps on his knee while staring straight ahead. William looks at his watch, then around the room and whistles The Star Spangled Banner.

ED: So . . . how does it feel?

WILLIAM: How does what feel?

ED: You know what I'm talking about.

WILLIAM: Well . . . I'm kinda . . . I'm happy. I'm very happy.

ED: (*hyper*) That's it, just happy? Bull! Come on man, what are you feeling right now?

WILLIAM: Scared shitless.

The door opens and Andre enters.

WILLIAM: I don't know. I'm a little worried that maybe we're rushing things a bit. Maybe we should have lived together first. (*a beat*) Aw, what the fuck am I saying. She's the best thing that has ever happened to me. I don't know why I'm getting cold feet.

ANDRE: It's only natural to get cold feet. It's better to get cold feet and change your mind than to go through with something that's not right.

WILLIAM: Nah, this is definitely the right thing for me. I'm ready. It's time for me to settle down and get my life together.

ANDRE: You sure?

WILLIAM: I'm sure.

ANDRE: Tony Greene said he was sure and look at him now.

ED: Quit it Snake!

ANDRE: Tony hasn't been married six months and he's already back at the Ice hustlin' fly girls.

WILLIAM: True, true, but that's Tony. He's a sick bastard with a pregnant wife that he never wanted to marry. I'm making my own decisions. No pressure. No shotguns. That's the difference. No, the difference is that I love Eve.

ED: (*to Andre*) What about your brother Pete? He's happily married with three kids and a collie.

ANDRE: Pete's a fuckin' wimp. How can you compare Pete to Killer? Pete went out with that fat ugly wife of his for six years before he married her. She's the only woman he's ever had or could get. Shit, he's not smart enough to be unhappy.

WILLIAM: Neither am I.

ED: (*pissed*) What kind of best man are you, coming in here bad-mouthing marriage?

WILLIAM: It's alright, Ed. He's just being himself. It doesn't bother me. I know what I'm doing and I know what he's doing.

ANDRE: (*to Ed*) I'm just testing him to see if he's sure about this.

ED: Right.

ANDRE: Really.

Ed looks at his watch.

ED: Shit! People are going to start coming soon I'd better ...

ANDRE: (*rushing Ed out*) Yeah man, you'd better get up there.

Ed exits and closes the door behind him. Andre speaks anxiously to William.

ANDRE: Look, you can still get outa this. I got some money you can have. You can go to Atlantic City or someplace and lay low. In a couple'a weeks everyone will have forgotten all about this.

WILLIAM: You never quit, do you?

ANDRE: (*retreating*) I'm just bullshittin'.

WILLIAM: Sure. (*Troy enter humming Here Comes The Bride.*) I thought you said you wouldn't be here 'til later.

TROY: Yeah, well, I left services early so I could make it over here on time.

WILLIAM: (*sincerely*) Thanks a lot Tr...Israel. I really appreciate it.

TROY: Well, I...

ANDRE: Yo man, where's your beanie? I thought that was part of the new you.

TROY: To tell the truth you won't be seeing me wearing a yarmulke anymore.

WILLIAM: Why not?

TROY: I won't be returning to the synagogue.

WILLIAM: What happened?

TROY: Last night I stayed up quite late studying the scripture and so I overslept this morning and as a result I was slightly tardy for today's service. Consequently, when I arrived the Rabbi had already begun pontificating about the importance of a literal interpretation of the Old Testament and I had to forego my usual front pew for a folding chair in the rear. Anyway, I was quite sleepy and the Rabbi's monotone monologue lulled me into the arms of Morpheus. After a short slumber, I was awakened by a blood-curdling scream. I opened my eyes and discovered the good Rabbi performing circumcisions on grown men. I immediately knew it was time for a quick decision. I thought a moment and I realized that after seventeen years, I have grown quite attached to my foreskin and therefore decided it was time to seek spiritual guidance elsewhere.

WILLIAM: A wise decision, my friend.

I think so. Anyway, enough said about me. How are you? You nervous?

WILLIAM: A little.

ANDRE: A little?

TROY: Remember when Pete got married? He was a nervous wreck. I've never seen anyone perspire as profusely as Pete. His hands were trembling and he started stuttering again. Remember that? You know, I almost got married once.

ANDRE: Right.

TROY: No, really. Remember when I was a member of Rev. Moon's church?

WILLIAM: Who could forget?

TROY: During that time I was spiritually matched with a beautiful young Korean girl named Kim Lee Washington. She was half Korean and half African American. The most beautiful woman I've ever met. Anyway, we were paired off to be married, but she changed her mind and left the church.

Pause. William and Andre look at Troy and then at each other. Andre rolls his eyes.

ANDRE: Okay, why did she leave the church?

TROY: Because we were told that we had to abstain from getting to know each other, in the biblical sense that is, for the entire first year of our marriage. I understood how celibacy could contribute to our continued spiritual growth, but Kim wanted to consummate our union immediately after the wedding. We argued. She left.

ANDRE: You're bullshittin'!

TROY: Yeah, I am. (*a beat*) But I did actually fall in love with Kim during that time. She had the most beautiful hazel eyes. She was from Staten Island. That ruined it. How could I have a relationship with a girl from Staten Island? Forget about the commute, think about how difficult it would have been for our children. One parent from Queens, the other from Staten Island. Think of the stigma, the torment, the jokes. It would almost be as bad as being from New Jersey.

ANDRE: Man, don't you have something to do?

Troy looks at his watch.

TROY: I guess I ought to go help Ed. Later. (*He goes out the door, closes it behind him, then pops his head back in and speaks.*) I'll see you on the other side of the broom.

WILLIAM: Huh?

TROY: After you jump it.

WILLIAM: Oh yeah, see you out there.

Troy exits.

ANDRE: What was that about?

WILLIAM: I dunno. (*He looks at his watch.*) Soon it'll be all over but the crying.

ANDRE: Yeah. You'll be starting a whole new way of life. No more just doing shit at the spur of the moment . . . (*short pause*) . . . Killer, you ever think about how little you really know about Eve? A year ago you didn't even know her and now you're about to commit your life to her. Like, what do you know a bout the kind of people she used to hang out with before you met her?

WILLIAM: Damn, you're starting to sound like my mother! What fuckin' difference does it make? I love her. She loves me and that's all I need to know!

ANDRE: I just want to make sure you know what you're getting into, that's all.

WILLIAM: I know what I'm doing, okay?

ANDRE: Okay.

Andre is now sitting, and William paces in front of him. There is silence for a few moments, then the wedding processional is heard in the background. Andre stands and William continues to pace.

ANDRE: Look, I gotta tell you something. I can't keep it to myself anymore. (*Andre pauses, expecting William to stop pacing.*) Listen to me man! You know you're my boy. I would never purposely hurt you. You're my best friend. I just...I just...I just...never thought things would happen like this. Damn it, stand still and listen to me!

William turns and punches Andre in the face, knocking him to the floor.

WILLIAM: (*calmly*) No muthafucka, you listen to me. I know. You feel better now? Why couldn't you just leave it alone? Shit, it's a little late to get a fuckin' conscience. Did you think this was gonna be like a fuckin' confession? Did you think I'd just make you say twenty hail-Marys and everything would be hunky dory?

(*Pause. William shakes his head.*)
I can't believe I was gonna let you think you got over free and easy. Do you believe that? That's the kind of guy I am. When we were kids my mother always asked me why I liked you. She thought you were bad and I was so good. I remember all the fights I got into because of you. But I always had your back. If Snake got his ass kicked, so did Killer. You fuck with one, you fuck with both.

ANDRE: I'm sorry man.

Andre gets up and sits on a chair and stares at the floor.

WILLIAM: What happened? What did I ever do to make you do this to me? Come on, let's have it. How could you?

ANDRE: (*very upset, near tears*) I didn't mean to ... I mean, I didn't know you were this serious. You never ...

WILLIAM: You no good sonofabitch! (*He grabs Andre by the shirt and stands him up.*) I ought to beat the shit outa you!

William pushes Andre into the wall where the chairs are and turns away shaking his head.

ANDRE: I'm sorry man. I'm sorry.

WILLIAM: Yeah, right. You're sorry because you blew it. Fucked yourself right into a corner. I know you think I hate you. I don't hate you. Really, I don't. I pity you. You know why? Because I'm gonna make you live with this. I'm gonna marry Eve and you're gonna be the best man. My kids will call you Uncle Andre. I might even name a son after you. Wouldn't that be some shit? We'll go bowling on Wednesday nights and you'll bring me home when I'm too drunk to drive. Shit, we'll be old men together and everyone will say "What great fuckin' friends those old guys are." And one day I'll die and you'll be left to think about all the good times and all the shit we did together. And you'll think about what you did to me. And that's when you'll really be sorry.

(*William looks at his watch. He then straightens Andre's bow tie.*) Well homeboy ... (*He grabs Andre's face and kisses him on the lips. Andre stands frozen.*) ... it's show time!

William opens the door and walks out, leaving the door open.

Very slow fade to black.

The end.

BIOGRAPHICAL/BIBLIOGRAPHICAL NOTES

Salimah Ali lives in Jamaica (Queens). She's been doing photography for seventeen years. Among her publication credits are *Ms. Magazine*, *Essence*, *Black Enterprise* and *Our Town News*. She's exhibited widely, at the Museum of Fine Arts in Massachusetts, the Studio Museum in Harlem, and elsewhere, and her work has been featured in several documentary volumes on photography.

Julia Alvarez spent her early childhood in the Dominican Republic, the birthplace of both her parents. Her family came to the United States when she was ten years old. In Queens, they had their own house in Jamaica. "That experience of a new world, language, way of making meaning, spurred me on to become a writer." Her books include *Homecoming* (poems; Grove Press, 1984) and *How The Garcia Girls Lost Their Accents*, a novel-in-stories (Algonquin Books of Chapel Hill, 1991). She teaches English and creative writing at Middlebury College, and is at work on a new novel.

Joseph Barbato was born in Jackson Heights, and lives outside Washington, D. C., where he is an editorial director at the international headquarters of The Nature Conservancy and a contributing editor with *Publishers Weekly*. He is the grandson of an Italian cigarmaker, an Irish maid, and a German burlesque comedian. Barbato was a senior writer and communications manager at N.Y.U. and the City University of New York, and a full-time freelance contributor to publications ranging from *Smithsonian* and *The New York Times* to *The Progressive* and *The Village Voice*. He's a member of the Authors Guild and the National Book Critics Circle. He and Lisa Weinerman Horak edited *Heart Of The Land* (Pantheon, 1995). He's writing a book about Elmhurst, Queens.

Mohamad Bazzi has lived in Jackson Heights ever since he left

215

his native Lebanon in 1985. He's a staff writer for *New Youth Connections*, and a frequent contributor to *New York Newsday*. He's also worked at the *Western Queens Gazette*, the *Woodside Herald*, and the *Queens Tribune*.

Clark Blaise lived in Astoria. His parents are French-Canadian. He is the Director of the International Writing Program at the University of Iowa. Some of his most recent books are: a collection of stories, *Man And His World* (Porcupine's Quill, Toronto, 1992), and an autobiography, *I Had A Father* (Addison-Wesley, 1993).

Javier Castano was born, and grew up in, Bogota, Colombia. He lives in Astoria, and has lived in Woodside, Corona and Sunnyside. In New York, he studied photo-journalism, and is working at *El Diario/La Prensa* newspaper, writing about the Hispanic community and the city.

Hsiang-Shui Chen lived in Flushing, and is now back in Taiwan, where he was born. His paper, "Toward a History of Chinese in Queens" (1989), excerpted here, is part of a series, "Working Papers," put out by the Asian/American Center at Queens College.

A.J. Cipolla was born in 1951, and has lived in Maspeth, Elmhurst and Ozone Park. He now lives in Red Hook, New York, and writes novels, plays, songs and screenplays. He's a house-husband rearing three children, ten, nine and two. Both sides of his family came from Italy.

Norman Clarke lives in Bellerose, lived in Astoria, Elmhurst, Jackson Heights and Woodside. He was born in England in 1950, came to New York in 1958. He's married, has three children, and is a commercial artist.

Mario M. Cuomo was born in South Jamaica (Queens). His

parents came from Salerno, Italy. He was the governor of the State of New York. His piece in this book is from a speech of his that is excerpted in his Introduction to *Diaries Of Mario M. Cuomo* (Random House, 1984).

Joan Dobbie lives in Oregon. In Queens, she had lived in Jamaica. She was born in Switzerland in 1946. Her parents fled Hitler in Vienna in 1938. She teaches Hatha Yoga and poetry, and has two grown children.

Rodlyn H. Douglas was born in Trinidad and Tobago and came to the U.S.A. in 1967. She lives in Springfield Gardens with her husband and three children. Some publishing credits: *Erotique Noire/Black Erotica* (1992 antho., Bantam Doubleday Dell), *Creation Fire: Anthology of Caribbean Women Writers* (Sister Vision Press, Toronto, 1990), and *The New Voices* (T & T, 1990).

Didi Dubelyew lived in Flushing, and was given her first camera, a 1964 World's Fair souvenir, *at* that World's Fair, which was in Flushing Meadows. She lives in Florida. Her mother is from France. She's also a poet, the author of *when the sunset smelled like red zinger, summer sweats,* and *diary of a mad hatter.*

Ed DuRanté spent his first fifteen years growing up in Queens Village. He lives in the East Village of Manhattan, where he is a director/actor/writer. His plays include *Homeboys,* excerpted here and produced at St. Louis Black Repertory Company, *Spare Change,* and *The L Word,* which was produced at Theatre for the New City. He is also a rap artist with the band, Gemini & The Zodiac Killers.

Rhina Espaillat was born in the Dominican Republic in 1932. She lived in Flushing for thirty-eight years, and presently lives in Massachusetts. She was anthologized in *Looking For Home:*

Women Writing About Exile (Milkweed Editions, 1990), and just published her first full collection of poems, *Lapsing To Grace* (Bennett & Kitchel).

Audrey Gottlieb lives in Hunters Point/Long Island City, lived in Astoria, and has traveled a good deal through the other sixty-two towns in Queens. Her grandparents came from Ukraine, Poland and Hungary. She's an internationally recognized photojournalist who specializes in travel photography of Greece and Cyprus. Currently, she's documenting Queens neighborhoods, architecture and folklife.

Lisa Weinerman Horak just got married! See her note under "W".

Darryl Holmes lives in Jamaica (Queens). He is an alumnus of The Afrikan Poetry Theatre, and the recipient of the Gwendolyn Brooks Award for Poetry. His work has appeared in *Obsidian II*, *The Small Press Reader* and other publications, and his first collection of poetry, *Wings Will Not Be Broken*, was published by Third World Press in 1990.

Thomas E. Kennedy was born in Flushing, grew up in Elmhurst, and lived also in Woodside and Jackson Heights. He's been living in Denmark for eight years. His family came from Ireland, France and Germany. He spent the bulk of his summers on the beach at Rockaway and playing handball and three-card monty in the P.S. 89 schoolyard. His books include a novel, *Crossing Borders* (Watermark, 1990).

Rudy Kikel grew up in Glendale and lived in Astoria. He now lives in Massachusetts. His parents came from Austria. Books: *Lasting Relations* (SeaHorse, 1984) and *Long Division* (Writers Block Co., 1992), the latter of which also contained "Necessary Relocations," which appears here. He's an editor of *Bay Windows*, a weekly gay and lesbian newspaper.

Yala Korwin is from Kew Gardens Hills. She was born in Poland. She's the author of *Tell The Story: Poems of the Holo-*

caust (Holocaust Publications, 1987), and has published in *Bitterroot*, in which "America! America!" first appeared, *Phoebus, Piedmont Literary Review* and elsewhere, including some anthologies.

Corky Lee lives in Astoria, and has lived in St. Albans, Hollis, Jamaica and Elmhurst. His family comes from the People's Republic of China. His business card reads: "Undisputed, Unofficial Asian American Photographer Laureate." His work has been shown in Boston, New York, San Francisco, Denver, Honolulu, Beijing, Tokyo and elsewhere, and published in *Time, The New York Times*, and *China Daily*, as well as carried by The Associated Press.

David Low grew up in Ridgewood. His parents came from China. Now he's living in Manhattan, New York. "Winterblossom Garden" was first published in 1982 in *The Ploughshares Reader: New Fiction for the Eighties*, and was anthologized in the 1989 New American Library's *American Families*. His stories have appeared in *Kansas Quarterly, Mississippi Review* and elsewhere.

Jaime Manrique was born in Colombia, has lived in Jackson Heights, and lives in Manhattan. His novel, *Latin Moon In Manhattan*, was published by St. Martin's Press in 1992. "Colombian Queens" is from that. His first volume of poetry received Colombia's National Poetry Award.

Maureen McCafferty lives in Glendale, and has lived in Rego Park, Forest Hills and Astoria. Her family is from Ireland. Her recently-published stories have appeared in *Arizona Mandala* and *American Writing*, and two are forthcoming in *Rhino* and *Encodings*. She has a Doctor of Arts from Syracuse University's Writing Program.

Susan Montez will be back in Astoria, from Chase City, Virginia where she was teaching high school English, when this book is out. Her family came from Czechoslovakia and England. Her work has appeared in *Hampden-Sydney Poetry Review*, *Puerto del Sol*, *Artful Dodge*, *Long Shot* and other places. Poems of hers were recently accepted by *Poetry East*, *Cream City Review* and *13th Moon*. She and we are talking about our bringing out her collection titled *Radio Free Queens*.

Bharati Mukherjee lived in Astoria. She was born in India, and is presently living in Iowa. "Danny's Girls" is from her 1988 Grove Press collection, *The Middleman And Other Stories*, which won the National Book Critics Circle Award.

Mark Nickerson lived in Hunters Point/Long Island City, and presently lives in Scarsdale, New York. His family is from England, France and Germany. He's exhibited his photographs in the past few years at Synchronicity Space in SoHo, Cortland Jessup Gallery in Provincetown, The Hunters Point Artists Community's tour/exhibition, and elsewhere. He curated a traveling exhibit called "Dirty Realism" in 1991.

Susan Orlean grew up in Cleveland, and attended the University of Michigan. Her family comes from Poland and Hungary. She's been a staff writer at *The New Yorker* since 1987. Her book, *Saturday Night* (Knopf, 1990) is about Saturday nights in eighteen communities, large and small, around the United States.

Silvio Martinez Palau was born in Colombia in 1954. He's lived in Woodside and Astoria since 1967. He has a Masters in Romance Languages from Queens College, and in Translation from New York University. He teaches high school Spanish. A collection of his short stories, *Made In USA*, was published in 1986 by Ediciones del Norte. His play, *The English Only Restaurant*, which is excerpted here, was produced by The Puerto Rican Traveling Theater of New York and The Kennedy Center in Washington, D.C., and published by Samuel French of London and New York in 1992.

Roger Sanjek lived in Fresh Meadows, and now lives in Manhattan. His family came from Yugoslavia. His paper, "The People of Queens from Now to Then," excerpted here, was presented at a conference, "350 Years of Life in Queens," in 1988. He is a founder of the Asian/American Center at Queens College.

Daniel Schweikert was born in 1934 in Middle Village, where he lived until 1955. He lives in New Jersey with his wife and four daughters, and does free-lance writing on a variety of subjects. His family came from Germany and Ireland.

Virginia Montero Seplowin lived in Astoria and Long Island City, and now lives in Manhattan. Her parents came from Puerto Rico. She has a doctorate in social work, and taught at the University of Puerto Rico, where she researched her geneology and now plans to write it.

Morty Sklar, co-editor of this collection, was born in 1935 in Sunnyside, grew up in Elmhurst, and lived in Jackson Heights from then on except for eighteen years in Iowa City (until 1989). His father fled the Russian Czar in 1907, and his mother's parents came from Poland and Austria. "Smoke" was first published in his collection of poems, *The Night We Stood Up For Our Rights* (The Toothpaste Press, 1977). In Iowa City, he founded The Spirit That Moves Us Press in 1975.

Barbara Unger lived in Woodside and Jackson Heights. Now she lives in Suffern, New York. Her family came from Poland, Russia and Austria. Her stories and poems about her childhood in Queens have appeared in *Midstream*, *Jewish Currents*, *Reconstructionist*, *Crazyquilt*, and in "Blue Depression Glass" from *Troika One* (Thorntree Press, 1991).

Harvey Wang was born in Clearview, grew up in Rosedale and lived in Sunnyside. He lives in Brooklyn. His family is from Austria, Hungary, and Poland. These photographs are from his book, *Harvey Wang's New York* (W.W. Norton, 1990). He's a free-lancer who's worked for such publications as *The Village Voice* and *New York*, and showed his work at the Museum of the City of New York and elsewhere. His subjects "are not the neon but the bedrock of society."

Lisa Weinerman Horak just got married—which is one reason her name isn't listed under "H" (the other reason is, this book is not typeset with a computer). She "is, regrettably, not from Queens." She grew up in Baltimore. Her family is of Polish and Russian descent. She lives in Arlington, Virginia and works at The Nature Conservancy, "where she foolishly believes she can change the world." She is co-editor, with Joseph Barbato, of *Heart Of The Land* (Pantheon, 1995).

Didi S. DubelyeW, photographer